FREE VIDEO  **FREE VIDEO**

PHR Essential Test Tips Video from Trivium Test Prep!

Dear Customer,

Thank you for purchasing from Trivium Test Prep! We're honored to help you prepare for your PHR exam.

To show our appreciation, we're offering a **FREE *PHR Essential Test Tips* Video by Trivium Test Prep**.* Our video includes 35 test preparation strategies that will make you successful on the PHR. All we ask is that you email us your feedback and describe your experience with our product. Amazing, awful, or just so-so: we want to hear what you have to say!

To receive your **FREE *PHR Essential Test Tips* Video**, please email us at 5star@ triviumtestprep.com. Include "Free 5 Star" in the subject line and the following information in your email:

1. The title of the product you purchased.
2. Your rating from 1 – 5 (with 5 being the best).
3. Your feedback about the product, including how our materials helped you meet your goals and ways in which we can improve our products.
4. Your full name and shipping address so we can send your **FREE *PHR Essential Test Tips* Video**.

If you have any questions or concerns please feel free to contact us directly at 5star@trivium-testprep.com.

Thank you!

- Trivium Test Prep Team

*To get access to the free video please email us at 5star@triviumtestprep.com, and please follow the instructions above.

PHR® Study Guide 2021–2022

Exam Prep Book with Practice Test Questions for the Professional in Human Resources Certification

TABLE OF CONTENTS

INTRODUCTION

Congratulations on choosing to take the PHR® or SPHR®! By purchasing this book, you've taken the first step toward becoming a certified Professional in Human Resources or Senior Professional in Human Resources!

This guide will provide you with a detailed overview of the PHR® and SPHR® so you know exactly what to expect on test day. We'll take you through all the concepts covered on the test and give you the opportunity to test your knowledge with practice questions. Even if it's been a while since you last took a major test, don't worry; we'll make sure you're more than ready!

WHAT ARE THE PHR® AND SPHR®?

The HR Certification Institute (HRCI)

The internationally recognized HR Certification Institute (HRCI) offers these exams, having certified over 130,000 HR professionals around the world. Certification by the HRCI is a globally recognized demonstration of professional achievement.

The different types of certification exams available from HRCI include Professional in Human Resources (PHR®), Senior Professional in Human Resources (SPHR®), Global Professional in Human Resources (GPHR®), and more. This study guide focuses on preparing candidates for PHR® and SPHR® certifications.

PHR® Certification

PHR® certification is appropriate for department-oriented HR professionals who execute specific HR duties, implement HR programs, and report to more senior HR professionals. Certification requires knowledge of applicable employment laws and regulations, and mastery of the technical aspects of HR.

SPHR® Certification

SPHR® certification is appropriate for HR professionals in management roles with a strategic, organizational perspective. SPHR® candidates already have a deep knowledge of all HR functions; they manage the HR department, design programs, and collaborate with organizational leaders.

Eligibility Requirements

Both certifications have different basic requirements:

Eligibility for PHR® and SPHR® Certification

PHR®	SPHR®
A master's degree with a minimum of one year of experience in an exempt-level (professional) HR position, OR	At least four years of experience in an exempt-level (professional) HR position with a master's degree at minimum, OR
A bachelor's degree and a minimum of two years of experience in an exempt-level (professional) HR position, OR	A bachelor's degree and a minimum of five years of experience in an exempt-level (professional) HR position, OR
A minimum of four years of experience in an exempt-level (professional) HR position with at least a high school diploma	A minimum of seven years of experience in an exempt-level (professional) HR position with at least a high school diploma

WHAT'S ON THE PHR® AND SPHR®?

Both certifications cover essentially the same content; however the tests differ slightly in their emphasis. HRCI designs each certification exam based on knowledge determined by HR practitioners around the world. HR tasks and the knowledge needed to perform them are extensively researched and grouped into functional areas, detailed below. The book will review this content to prepare you for the exam.

Body of Knowledge Required for PHR®/SPHR® Certification

PHR®	SPHR®
Business Management (20%)	Leadership and Strategy (40%)
Talent Planning and Acquisition (16%)	Talent Planning and Acquisition (16%)
Learning and Development (10%)	Learning and Development (12%)
Total Rewards (15%)	Total Rewards (12%)
Employee and Labor Relations (39%)	Employee Relations and Engagement (20%)

HOW ARE THE PHR® AND SPHR® SCORED AND ADMINISTERED?

The PHR® and SPHR® exams are computer-based, three-hour exams. Each exam consists of 175 multiple-choice questions, of which 150 are scored and twenty-five are pre-test, unscored questions. Each question lists four possible answer choices. Only one answer choice is correct.

You will receive a preliminary score immediately after you complete the computer-based exam. HRCI will send your official results and score to you within two to four weeks. You will need a scaled score of at least 500 to pass.

- Be sure to register for an exam by the established deadlines listed at www.hrci.org.
- Give yourself several weeks to study and develop a study schedule to break up the information into manageable chunks.
- Find a study group or have a friend quiz you on HR knowledge.
- Get acquainted with the testing facility rules and check-in procedures.

- Give yourself plenty of time to find the test site. Plan to arrive early.
- Arrive at least thirty minutes prior to your scheduled exam time. Bring a valid, government-issued photo ID.

ABOUT TRIVIUM TEST PREP

Trivium Test Prep uses industry professionals with decades' worth of knowledge in their fields, proven with degrees and honors in law, medicine, business, education, the military, and more, to produce high-quality test prep books for students.

Our study guides are specifically designed to increase any student's score, regardless of his or her current skill level. Our books are also shorter and more concise than typical study guides, so you can increase your score while significantly decreasing your study time.

HOW TO USE THIS GUIDE

This guide is not meant to waste your time on superfluous information or concepts you've already learned. Instead, this guide will help you master the most important test topics and also develop critical test-taking skills. To support this effort, the guide provides:

- organized concepts with detailed explanations
- practice questions with worked-through solutions
- key test-taking strategies
- simulated one-on-one tutor experience
- tips, tricks, and test secrets

Because we have eliminated the filler and fluff, you'll be able to work through the guide at a significantly faster pace than you would with other test prep books. By allowing you to focus only on those concepts that will increase your score, we'll make your study time shorter and more effective.

BUSINESS MANAGEMENT, STRATEGY, AND LEADERSHIP

SECTION OVERVIEW

- What is strategic management, and why is it important?
- How are organizations structured?
- What are the main functions within most organizations?
- What external factors affect how an organization is run?
- How do organizations develop and change over time?
- What is the strategic planning process, and what does it achieve?
- How is HR involved in the strategic planning process?
- How do organizations manage change?
- How do companies ensure that their practices are ethical?
- What is organizational design, and how does it affect decision-making?
- What are the different approaches to leadership?
- What is the role of human resources in the organization?
- What is the difference between a generalist and a specialist?
- How can HR professionals collaborate with business leaders?
- Why do organizations develop HR policies and procedures?
- How do HR professionals use technology to accomplish their goals and objectives?
- How do HR professionals use data analysis to collaborate with leadership?
- What is the role of HR in mergers and acquisitions?

WHAT IS STRATEGIC MANAGEMENT?

Over the past century, companies have grown larger and more complicated as the demands of consumers and the business environment have grown more complex and nuanced. Products are now created using elaborate processes with multiple workers and machines. Additionally, as the US economy has evolved from primarily manufacturing products to providing services, companies have evolved to accommodate demand and trends and to stay competitive. Over time, companies have developed new processes, restructured their personnel, adopted new tools, and reevaluated management practices to ensure that their employees are able to achieve these overarching goals.

To stay competitive in a continually evolving global marketplace, business leaders must be able to quickly respond and adapt to change in the industry, economy, workforce, and regulatory environment. They must know needs of their clients and customers and develop useful products and services to meet those needs. Successful business leaders continually scan the environment, make predictions, and develop business plans accordingly to stay competitive. This ongoing process of creation, research, reassessment, and development is called **STRATEGIC MANAGEMENT.** Strategic management is important to human resources professionals because it affects how HR adds value to the organization through policies, procedures, and programs.

Strategic HR management, then, is achieved when HR leaders and practitioners closely align themselves with the overall strategic management of the company. Since organizations are comprised of people, the human resources function is affected by anything that affects all people in the organization. When the organization must respond to changes in the marketplace, industry, or regulatory environment, HR practitioners are responsible for aligning the organization's people, policies, and processes with these changes. To be successful in doing so, they must collaborate with business leadership to stay aware of business goals, objectives, and strategic vision.

Various Structures of Organizations

Every company is organized differently depending on factors like industry, size, tax implications, leadership, and others. However, all businesses operating in the United States are formally organized into one of four basic structures[1]. **SOLE PROPRIETORSHIPS** are the most basic business structure. In sole proprietorships, the business owner operates alone as the sole responsible party for the business (including finances); he or she has the sole authority to make business decisions. Any profits made by the business belong to the owner, and the owner is personally responsible for all debts and liabilities of the company. Many business owners of a sole proprietorship operate the company through an assumed name registered with the county or state in which they operate.

A **PARTNERSHIP** in contrast is a business structure in which two or more people share ownership. Partnerships may take various forms such as a general partnership, limited liability partnership, or a joint venture, depending on the structure of ownership as well as the intended duration of the partnership. Formal agreements in many partnerships specify division of profits, dispute resolution, changes in ownership, and dissolution of the partnership. Third, a **CORPORATION** is an entity owned by shareholders (in the form of stock or equity). Corporations, not their owners (shareholders) are legally responsible, or liable, for the company's debts and actions—unlike partnerships and sole proprietorships. Shareholders are typically not involved in the daily operations of the business. Instead, they elect a board of directors to represent their interests, and the company's senior leadership team makes decisions about the direction of the company.

Finally, a corporation and a partnership can combine to create a **LIMITED LIABILITY COMPANY (LLC)**. As with corporations, LLCs offer their owners, called members, protection from liability; furthermore, they offer the simplified tax structure of a partnership. There may be one or more members of an LLC.

Operational Functions in an Organization

Regardless of size and formal structure, most organizations need certain **CORE FUNCTIONS** to operate. Below are the general business functions that contribute to achieving the organization's objective[2]:

- Procurement, Logistics, and Distribution professionals acquire resources (inputs) and deliver final products to customers.

- Product or Service Development professionals design, revise, and improve products or services offered to the marketplace; their duties may include research, design, analysis, and engineering.

- Operations professionals and teams organize raw products and production processes to create a final product or service; they also determine methods for cost savings.

- Marketing and Sales professionals target prospective clients, develop and maintain relationships with existing customers, and promote and advertise products and services through multiple channels.

- Customer Service representatives support customers who purchase products or services, resolve problems and complaints, and answer questions about products or services.

The following are support functions:

- General Management oversees corporate governance, accounting, facilities, management, and administrative support.
- Human Resources professionals oversees the recruitment, hiring, training, compensation, and termination of employees.
- Information Technology professionals maintain, automate, and design the technical infrastructure of the organization, including equipment, hardware, and software.

Depending on the complexity and size of the organization, these functions may be handled by one person or multiple people. All are necessary components for conducting business.

The External Environment

Regularly monitoring and responding to the EXTERNAL ENVIRONMENT is critical to the success of an organization. External forces such as the economy, consumer demand, laws and regulations, technology, and the labor force greatly affect the operations of an organization. Being proactive and adapting to these changes helps an organization remain strong. Of primary importance are economic conditions. When the economy is strong, consumers can afford more products and services; companies thrive if they meet the demands of consumers and often expand their staff in order to meet that demand. On the other hand, when the economy is stagnant or in decline, consumers purchase fewer products and services. Consequently, companies may respond by reducing production costs to offset the loss of profits; this may lead to reduction in staff. Consumer demand can affect economic conditions for companies as demand for specific products increases or decreases. Over time, consumers develop new tastes, attitudes, and behaviors. What may have been useful for consumers a decade ago may not be today. Therefore, to meet consumer demand, companies refine their existing products and services, as well as develop new ones; this also affects staffing practices.

Organizations must also look beyond economics. The legal landscape is ever-changing; new laws and regulations are regularly implemented by local, state, and federal governments and agencies. These laws and regulations dictate how a company compensates employees, treats employees, and operates. Depending on where the company conducts business, it may have to follow rules in many different locations and therefore keep up with the changing legal landscape in each place. Meanwhile, it is strategically advantageous for organizations to stay abreast of developments in technology; they may benefit from new technology that streamlines operations and increases efficiency. Finally, it is in the best interests of the organization to attract the most qualified people to fulfill its goals and to remain a desirable place to work. The talent and skills of the individuals within the available workforce are critical to the success of organizations everywhere.

ORGANIZATIONAL CHANGE AND GROWTH

Like people, organizations have their own LIFE CYCLES. They are "born" (established), they develop and mature, they decline, and sometimes they "die" (dissolve). Just like people, as organizations mature, they begin to understand the environment around them, develop knowledge and wisdom, and plan for the future. Organizations at any stage of the life cycle are impacted by both internal and external factors. In order to survive, an organization must be able to adapt to changes, demands, and its internal and external environment.

According to the scholar Richard L. Daft, the expert in organization behavior and design, as an organization progresses through its life cycle and grows in size, its functions and features evolve over time:

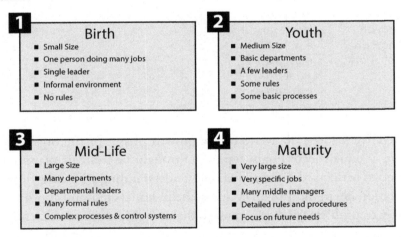

1 Birth
- Small Size
- One person doing many jobs
- Single leader
- Informal environment
- No rules

2 Youth
- Medium Size
- Basic departments
- A few leaders
- Some rules
- Some basic processes

3 Mid-Life
- Large Size
- Many departments
- Departmental leaders
- Many formal rules
- Complex processes & control systems

4 Maturity
- Very large size
- Very specific jobs
- Many middle managers
- Detailed rules and procedures
- Focus on future needs

Figure 1.1. The Life Cycle of a Company

Growth Phases

In 1972, organizational development scholar Larry E. Greiner conceptualized five GROWTH PHASES an organization undergoes: growth through creativity, direction, delegation, coordination, and collaboration. According to Greiner, each growth phase is a period of organizational evolution of four to eight years followed by a period of organizational crisis. The phases and the expected crises that result, according to his theory, are listed in greater detail in Table 1.1.

Table 1.1. Growth Phases of an Organization

GROWTH PHASE	RESULTING CRISIS	ORGANIZATIONAL NEEDS	ACTION TO BE TAKEN
growth through creativity	crisis of leadership	More formalized management practices are needed.	Leaders must adapt practices or hire managers to assume this authority.
growth through direction	crisis of autonomy	Lower level managers need more authority.	Leaders must delegate authority.
growth through delegation	crisis of control	Employees need autonomy to do jobs while leaders need to feel in control.	Leaders must develop a system of checks and balances.
growth through coordination	crisis of bureaucracy	Focus groups, planning processes, and staff cause delays in decision-making; innovation suffers.	Management must develop collaborative teams and break down silos.
growth through collaboration	No formal crisis is indicated. However, employees may grow exhausted by teamwork and pressure.		

Effective leaders are aware of the growth phases of the organization and plan accordingly, typically through the strategic planning process (discussed in detail below). Understanding where the organization lies in the growth cycle also helps leaders respond appropriately to problems and crises and to make decisions more efficiently. As organizations progress through the life cycle, it is important for leaders to manage change in order to ensure that management and staff are closely aligned with the strategic vision and objectives, in order for them to be carried out effectively.

Not all organizations are able to survive the growth phase in its entirety. Some may collapse due to an inability to respond to changes and demands. Others may be acquired by another company and therefore cease to operate autonomously. If an organization does successfully progress through the growth phases, it will reach a point of maturity and eventually decline.

Maturity and Decline

An organization has reached maturity once it has enough resources in order to plan for the future, and has formalized policies and procedures as well as a solid infrastructure in which it operates. In this stage of the organizational life cycle, it is typical for organizations to become bureaucratic, making it more difficult to make decisions or change direction quickly. Bureaucratization harms the organization if its competition or industry evolves at a rapid pace (e.g., by developing new products and services).

On the other hand, an organization in the maturity phase also experiences stability. Functional departments and formalized procedures make hiring and training staff easier. Additionally, mature organizations also have the financial resources and planning necessary to pay their employees competitively. The phase of maturity may last for several years or decades as long as the organization is able to respond to crises and changes in the environment.

Once an organization has reached a high level of inefficiency and bureaucracy, it will begin to decline. The organization's products or services may be outdated, and sales may decline, due to a lack of innovation. Leadership may respond by reducing the workforce, closing facilities, or finding other cost-cutting measures that reduce redundancy. In order to revive the organization, leaders must find a way to innovate by developing new or refined products or services that meet the demands of the marketplace. Otherwise, the organization may fail and cease to exist, or it may be acquired by a larger organization in a growth phase.

THE STRATEGIC PLANNING PROCESS

In order to respond to changes in the marketplace and continue to grow, organizations periodically undergo STRATEGIC PLANNING, a process of defining the overall purpose and goals of the organization and how these goals will be achieved. Through strategic planning, an organization determines its current status, direction, approach, and how it will measure its success. Strategic planning focuses on the organization as a whole rather than on a particular product or service. The process, which is generally carried out on a periodic basis, answers the following questions about the organization:

1. Where are we now?
2. Where do we want to be in _____ years?
3. How will we get there?
4. How will we know when we are there?

There are several approaches to strategic planning that may be tailored to the unique needs of the organization depending on its size, leadership, maturity level, and culture:

- Goals-based planning focuses on the organization's mission, vision, and values. Goals are set to achieve the mission; the steps needed to achieve the goals are determined.

- Issues-based planning focuses on the issues facing the organization and determines the steps needed to address those issues.

- Organic planning focuses on a common vision and values and identifying best practices and methodologies in the organization. The stakeholders focus on what is already working rather than fixing problems.

Regardless of the method, strategic plans are typically developed for a period of one year or more. Some plans may be in-depth, with step-by-step action plans, while others may be high-level with no specific steps. In general, though, the strategic planning process will have the following elements:

1. **PLAN THE PROCESS.** Stakeholders decide on process, participants, and time frame. Pre-planning reduces errors in the planning process and achieves commitment from leaders.

2. **STUDY THE ENVIRONMENT.** Stakeholders use tools such as statistical models, SWOT analysis, PEST analysis, and Porter's five forces to determine the organization's present state.

3. **FORMULATE A STRATEGY.** Stakeholders develop the organization's mission, vision, values, goals, and objectives; they focus on the future and the organization's direction or destination.

4. **IMPLEMENT THE STRATEGY.** Stakeholders articulate goals, develop budgets, create action plans, and execute plans.

5. **EVALUATE THE STRATEGY.** Stakeholders evaluate the strategy periodically and make adjustments.

The formal strategic plan, however, is not as important as the process itself, as well as the execution of the plan. An organization gains many benefits through the strategic planning process, including:

- creating a sense of purpose
- helping leadership set goals
- enhancing communication with staff
- keeping staff involved
- enabling leadership to allocate resources appropriately
- creating accountability
- building consensus

Statistical models analyze data to uncover trends affecting the organization.

SWOT analysis looks at an organization's internal Strengths and Weaknesses, and external Opportunities and Threats.

PEST analysis reviews how external Political, Economic, Social and Technological factors may impact an organization.

PORTER'S FIVE FORCES:

1. competition
2. the potential of new entrants to an industry
3. the power of suppliers
4. the power of customers
5. the threat of substitute products

These forces shape industries and show their strengths and weaknesses.

Uniting stakeholders to discuss the future of the organization is a healthy process that will keep it adaptable to change and viable in the marketplace. Leveraging the existing organizational hierarchy to execute the plan and reviewing progress periodically are keys to successfully implementing the strategic plan.

Mission, Vision, and Values

During the strategic planning process, an organization typically reviews its MISSION, VISION, and VALUES STATEMENTS. If the organization has not already created these, or is undergoing the process for the first time, it typically will develop these statements as part of the process. Once these statements are formalized, the organization develops goals to support them. These statements help stakeholders and employees maintain focus during the strategic planning process and throughout the year.

A **mission statement** defines the purpose of an organization, what it offers, whom it serves, and where it operates.

A **vision statement** outlines the goals of an organization.

An organization's **core values** are the values that frame its perspective and guide its actions.

Developing Goals

An organization's goals should be **SMART**:

- **S**pecific—goals must be clear and detailed enough to guide action plans.
- **M**easurable—goals require metrics to determine their progress.
- **A**ction-oriented—goals should describe the actions needed to accomplish them.
- **R**ealistic—goals should be achievable.
- **T**ime-based—goals require a timeframe for completion.

Implementing the Strategic Plan

Once the strategic plan has been developed, organizational leaders will consult with department heads, management, and other key employees to begin the implementation process. This process includes the development of tactical goals and action plans, which can be specific to departments, work groups, or even certain individuals in the organization. The tactical goals and action plans should tie directly to the more broadly stated strategic plan and should be SMART.

After the goals and action plans are developed, leadership and management will address budgetary issues and resources needed to achieve the strategic plan. The organization may decide it needs additional personnel, new technology, or external assistance. Those involved in the budgeting process will make recommendations on what cash and resources are needed, and leadership will determine whether these recommendations support the strategic plan.

Evaluating the Strategic Plan

Strategic planning does not end with the development of that plan. Rather, it is a continual process that occurs throughout the year or years. As the organization implements its plan, it should periodically evaluate whether it is on track to achieve the strategic goals. This would include evaluating the tactical goals and action plans as well. If the organization's leaders find that the organization is not on track, they may decide to revise the action plan or tactical goals or even to re-evaluate the strategic plan itself. Sometimes, internal or external factors may cause an organization to change course. Those organizations that are able to adapt accordingly to their environment are likely to succeed.

The Role of HR in Strategic Planning

Human resource leaders have an important role in the strategic planning process. HR develops its own goals and action plans that align with the overarching goals of the organization. The strategic HR plan—or HUMAN CAPITAL PLAN—addresses the same questions used during the larger strategic planning process. As with any strategic plan, the strategic HR plan will differ from organization to organization. However, there are some commonalities, as outlined in the following table:

Table 1.2. Components of a Human Capital Plan[3]

COMPONENT	EXPLANATION
strategic direction	Strategic direction requires knowledge of the organization's strategic plans, budgetary constraints, internal and external forces affecting human capital, makeup of the current workforce, and customer and stakeholder expectations, challenges, and needs. HR must develop a vision of the future workforce to determine the ideal human capital necessary for the organization to achieve its strategic goals.
human capital goals	Human capital goals are related to the organization's talent (employees), performance management, and leadership. Goals may relate to the hiring, training, and allocation of employees to achieve certain objectives in the organization's general strategic plan.
strategies for accomplishing goals	These strategies specifically describe how goals will be achieved. Consideration should be given to the availability and capabilities of human capital.

COMPONENT	EXPLANATION
implementation plan	The implementation plan describes the actions needed to accomplish goals and objectives. Implementation plans include the following components: - a description of each task necessary to carry out the objectives - stakeholders responsible for each task - resources required (e.g., human, financial) - timeframes (e.g., milestones, deadlines)
communications plan	The communications plan describes how key stakeholders in the organization will stay informed about the progress of the strategic plan and the actions they need to take. HR must communicate regularly with all stakeholders to ensure their understanding of the plan and to solicit feedback. The communications plan is often a subset of the implementation plan.

Once human resources leadership establishes a human capital management plan, it will then develop a budget to support the implementation of this plan. Depending on finances, the human resources departmental budget may include these costs:

- employee compensation (salaries, bonuses, and benefits)
- payroll taxes
- equipment and supplies
- training and development fees
- travel
- outsourced services (e.g., payroll, benefits administration, HRIS)

HR may also lead the development of budgetary items that are then allocated to other departments or verticals in the organization. These costs may include:

- recruitment fees
- training and development fees
- raises
- employee incentives or awards
- temporary staff

In some cases, it may be more cost-effective to outsource functions or repurpose HR positions to carry out new or different tasks. Furthermore, some processes may be streamlined so that HR personnel can focus their efforts on tasks that are more impactful to the organization.

Managing Organizational Change

As a result of the strategic planning process, an organization may decide that it needs to restructure itself in order to achieve its goals and remain competitive and viable in the marketplace. Organizational leadership may decide to explore or implement any of a number of structural changes.

In RESTRUCTURING or re-engineering, leadership may examine processes for redundancy within the entire organization or in certain departments or teams; it may also simplify operations in order to improve efficiency and reduce costs. With an EXPANSION IN FORCE, an organization grows teams by creating new positions and hiring additional personnel. This may lead to a culture clash between veteran employees and newcomers. It will also require resources to train the new employees and acclimate them to the new environment. Conversely, a REDUCTION IN FORCE decreases personnel expense by eliminating positions or departments. Also called DOWNSIZING, this may create anxiety for remaining employees, who must take on the extra workload while feeling uncertain about the security of their own jobs.

MERGERS AND ACQUISITIONS are a combination of two or more entities. In a merger, two companies combine to leverage both of their assets while forming a new, stronger corporate identity. Acquisitions involve a larger company purchasing another company and integrating it into the existing culture and operations. With DIVESTITURE, a company's product line, service, or business unit is spun off or sold. Typically, the existing team involved in the divestiture remains intact.

In OUTSOURCING, the organization uses external service providers to handle certain business functions, such as accounting, payroll, or IT. Finally, OFFSHORING is when an organization moves certain jobs or functions to other countries where labor is cheaper in order to achieve cost savings. This has other implications, such as a loss of jobs elsewhere, cultural barriers, and time zone differences.

Employees are all affected by organizational change in some way. In some cases, their responsibilities may increase or change. Others may worry about losing their jobs, or lose them altogether. HR professionals help manage organizational change by establishing programs and communications to help employees understand changes, manage their emotions, and adapt to restructuring. It is important for the organization to communicate regularly with employees to keep them apprised of the changes, let them know how they are affected, and be truthful about the facts. If the organization is not truthful, or if employees perceive that information is being withheld from them, it risks losing longer-term employees with historical knowledge who might otherwise stay. Decreased productivity could be the consequence.

CORPORATE GOVERNANCE AND ETHICS

CORPORATE GOVERNANCE refers to the set of systems, principles and processes that guide everything a company does, including the relationships between its stakeholders (i.e., board of directors, management, and others).

Corporate governance is based on transparency, integrity, fairness, compliance, accountability, and responsibility. An active, independent board of directors provides corporate oversight and represents shareholders' interests. The board of directors typically includes inside directors (those who work for the organization) and outside directors (those who do not have an employment relationship with the organization). The board is elected by the shareholders (who are owners of the corporation). Management, including executives, are employees of the organization and oversee the daily operations of the organization.

A corporation, while a legal entity, cannot make a decision for itself. Instead, the board of directors and management make decisions for the organization. These stakeholders have a fiduciary responsibility to the organization, meaning that they should make decisions that are in the best interests of stakeholders and the organization's survival. Of course, this does not always happen in the real world. In response to corporate scandals in the early 2000s by Enron and WorldCom, among others, the Sarbanes-Oxley Act was enacted in 2002 to ensure that stakeholders in public corporations appropriately maintain and uphold their fiduciary responsibilities.

The Sarbanes-Oxley Act of 2002

The SARBANES-OXLEY ACT addresses unethical practices in public corporations and provides penalties for violations. Its provisions include the following:

1. The Public Company Accounting Oversight Board was developed to require all public accounting firms to register with the board, which could audit the company's records for compliance.

2. Standards were established to maintain the independent nature of auditors. Results of audits (including recommendations) are now provided directly to the audit committee of the organization's board of directors.

3. Standards for corporate responsibility were established, and the organization's chief executive is held accountable for the accuracy of filings with the Securities and Exchange Commission.

4. CEOs and CFOs are required to forfeit bonuses or gains through shares of stock for a one-year period when the

organization files a restatement of financial reports with the SEC due to misconduct.

5. Insider trading of stock is prohibited during pension fund blackout periods.

6. CFOs must satisfy certain ethical requirements.

7. Management officials who commit fraud or obstruct justice face criminal penalties.

8. Whistleblowers who report misconduct they reasonably believe to violate SEC regulations or federal laws are protected.

Corporate Ethics

Ethical behavior begins at the highest levels of an organization. When the organization's directors, officers, and managers show their commitment to behaving ethically, employees are prone to follow their example. Many organizations, whether or not they are subject to compliance with Sarbanes-Oxley, demonstrate their commitment to corporate responsibility by developing organization-wide ethics statements, values statements, and codes of conduct.

Within the CODE OF CONDUCT, the organization should indicate how conflicts of interest, insider information, and gifts should be handled. CONFLICTS OF INTEREST arise when an employee may personally benefit from the action of the organization. Typically, the employee is required to disclose potential conflicts of interest, and management will identify ways to avoid or mitigate the conflict. Gifts from vendors or clients to an employee in the organization are a type of conflict of interest identified in such a policy. Insider information can lead to a conflict of interest when the employee has access to information that the general public does not have. Using insider information to make decisions on the purchase or sale of stock is prohibited by law and carries criminal and civil penalties.

A **code of ethics** is an organization's ideals—what it wants to do when conducting business.

A **code of conduct** is what an organization expects from employees; it also lays out how those who violate this code will be disciplined.

Whistleblower Protection

Under the Sarbanes-Oxley Act, violations of securities laws or a breach of fiduciary duty must be reported to the chief legal officer or CEO of the organization. An organization's legal team (in-house or external counsel) must also report these violations to the organization's board of directors audit committee. The Sarbanes-Oxley Act provides protections for people who, in good faith, report suspected or witnessed wrongdoing. These people are called WHISTLEBLOWERS; they include people who report violations, assist those reporting violations, and who assist in investigations.

Whistleblower protections are regulated by the Department of Labor and the Occupational Safety and Health Administration (OSHA). Under OSHA regulations, an employer is prohibited from taking adverse action against whistleblowers, including termination of employment, reducing pay, discipline, intimidation, coercion, or any other type of retaliation. Publicly traded companies are required by Sarbanes-Oxley to establish confidential whistleblower complaints and to maintain those records according to the rules established in the law. Organizations that are not publicly traded (and therefore not subject to Sarbanes-Oxley) may elect, at their own will, to establish whistleblower policies and procedures in order to maintain an ethical workplace.

Ethics Officers

Organizations committed to maintaining ethical standards often choose a key person to serve as an ethics officer. The ethics officer may be a person at the executive level, the company's internal legal counsel, or the highest-ranking human resources professional. Ethics officers advise all employees in the organization on their obligations to maintain an ethical workplace, including acceptable and unacceptable conduct. They oversee the training of all employees on ethical matters; they also develop policies to maintain compliance with Sarbanes-Oxley (as applicable) and consistency with corporate values and ethics. Finally, ethics officers consult with other organizational leaders on ethical issues.

LEGAL COMPLIANCE

Compliance means different things depending on the company or industry. However all companies with employees must comply with federal and state employment laws like the Fair Labor Standards Act and Occupational Safety and Health Act. It is the responsibility of employers to understand all the laws that apply to their business in the location(s) where they operate. Companies should develop sound, well-documented policies and train employees to understand and follow them. There should also be procedures for handling employees who do not comply with a company policy (and may therefore be non-compliant with the law).

Not only must companies comply with laws, but they must also understand and follow REGULATIONS, specific directives with the same force of law enacted by federal agencies in order to execute acts of Congress. The Family and Medical Leave Act (FMLA) is an example of a law passed by Congress that resulted in regulations and procedures developed by the Department of Labor, the regulatory agency that implements the law. The Internal Revenue Service (IRS) also creates regulations that can affect employee payroll and benefits.

The Federal Rulemaking Process

The Administration Procedure Act outlines the method in which federal rules must be proposed, amended, and finalized. The following are the basic steps for promulgating a federal rule or regulation:

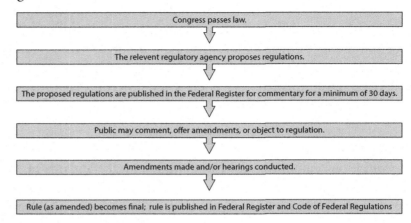

Congress passes law.

The relevent regulatory agency proposes regulations.

The proposed regulations are published in the Federal Register for commentary for a minimum of 30 days.

Public may comment, offer amendments, or object to regulation.

Amendments made and/or hearings conducted.

Rule (as amended) becomes final; rule is published in Federal Register and Code of Federal Regulations

Figure 1.2. The Federal Rulemaking Process

The applicable law (which the regulation supports) specifies the process used to create accompanying regulations. Some regulations require only publication and an opportunity for comments to become final. Others require publication and formal public hearings. Once a regulation becomes "final rule" and takes effect, it is published in the Federal Register, the Code of Federal Regulations (CFR), and on the website of the regulatory agency. Companies then must ensure **REGULATORY COMPLIANCE**.

ORGANIZATIONAL DESIGN AND DEVELOPMENT

Organizational design is the alignment of people, processes, compensation, and metrics with the strategy of the organization such that the organization embodies its core values as specified in its vision statement. The design reflects the organization's need to respond to changes (internal and external), integrate new people, technologies, and processes, encourage collaboration and offer flexibility. An organization can be organized in different ways, depending on its objectives. Leaders and managers must make decisions about how to group people together to perform their work effectively.

There are five common approaches to organizational design that help decision-makers group people (i.e., positions) together in the organization.

1. **FUNCTIONAL STRUCTURE** creates departments or units by organizing positions by tasks, expertise, skills, or resources. Groups within a functional structure could be accounting and finance, human resources, information technology, and marketing.

2. **DIVISIONAL STRUCTURE** groups business units according to a type of output. For example, units may be aligned with specific geographic locales, products, or clients.

3. **MATRIX STRUCTURE** mixes functional and divisional structure. People work in teams that integrate disparate expertise. Employees working in a matrix structure belong to both a functional and a divisional group (e.g., a project team or product team).

4. **TEAM STRUCTURE** integrates separate functions into a group based on a particular goal or objective. Teams foster collaboration, cooperation, problem solving, and relationship-building among various functions.

5. **NETWORK STRUCTURE** involves external entities performing certain functions on a temporary or contractual basis. Work is assigned, for example, to a contractor for a period of time in order to achieve a certain goal.

Organizational structures evolve over time due to organizational growth, environmental change, and other circumstances. The strategic planning process identifies ways to maintain a sound structure that position the organization to achieve its goals and objectives. The structure of the organization should support what the organization hopes to achieve. Otherwise, the organization will be at a disadvantage and may risk losing its competitiveness.

Centralized vs. Decentralized Decision-Making

In addition to the physical structure of the organization, it is important to consider the structure of decision-making. Decisions are constantly made in an organization: who to hire, what products or services to offer, where to operate, what clients to target and more. Decision-making in an organization can be either centralized or decentralized.

CENTRALIZED organizational structures depend on one individual (or group of executives) to make decisions and provide direction. Smaller organizations often use this structure because the owner is responsible for the company's business operations. As a benefit, centralized organizations often experience quick, efficient decision-making. Business owners typically set the company's mission, vision, goals, and objectives, which managers are expected to support and execute. However, centralized organizations can become bureaucratic as they grow, due to the hierarchy of management leading to the owner; accomplishing tasks takes longer, resulting in slower operations and lower productivity.

DECENTRALIZED organizational structures, on the other hand, often have several individuals responsible for management decisions. Decentralized organizations depend on a team environment at different levels of the business in order to make decisions. (Individuals may have some autonomy to make business decisions, but generally must be aligned with the vision of the larger group). Decentralized organizations typically employ individuals with a variety of knowledge and skills, ensuring that the company is positioned to handle various types of business situations. However, reaching consensus among decision-makers in decentralized organizations can be challenging. This can slow the organization's progress in achieving its objectives and harm productivity.

Organizational leadership should carefully consider work styles, personalities, goals, vision, and overall environment when deciding upon the right structure for the organization. Small organizations typically adopt centralized decision-making structures because owners often remain at the forefront of business operations. Larger organizations often utilize a more decentralized structure because they have several divisions or departments. Additionally, business leaders may need to consider changing organizational structure depending on the growth of the business and overall strategy.

Distribution and Coordination of Labor

Regardless of their structure, all organizations are groups of people working together toward a common goal. To efficiently accomplish their goals, organizations typically divide work into manageable parts. They also coordinate the work that employees do to ensure that everyone is working interdependently toward the same objectives.

DIVISION OF LABOR refers to the distribution of work into separate jobs that are performed by different people. Division of labor leads to JOB SPECIALIZATION as workers focus on one or a few tasks now essential to their positions. As companies grow over time, horizontal division of labor (i.e., many people doing similar jobs) is usually accompanied by a vertical division of labor (i.e., a hierarchy of managers and supervisors overseeing jobs performed). Job specialization also increases work efficiency. Workers can master smaller tasks quickly, and less time is wasted changing from one task to another. Training costs are also reduced because employees require fewer skills to accomplish the assigned work. Finally, job specialization makes it easier to recruit and hire people best suited for the specific jobs. However, an organization's ability to divide work among employees depends on how well those people can collaborate and work with one another. Otherwise, productivity suffers due to the misallocation of tasks or resources, or duplication of effort.

Coordination tends to become more challenging as jobs become more specialized. Therefore, companies typically specialize jobs to the point that coordination is possible. Every organization coordinates work via informal communication, formal hierarchy, or standardization. Informal communication includes sharing information with other employees via face-to-face interaction, email, and conference calls. Team meetings are a common source of informal communication, where tactical matters are discussed and work is coordinated at a more specific level. Hierarchy gives authority to individuals at certain levels of the organization, who then direct work processes and allocate resources. This is also known as the chain of command. Standardization is the development of routine processes, measured outputs, and required training or competencies.

Span of Control

SPAN OF CONTROL describes the extent of a manager's authority: the amount of employees reporting to him or her. If only a few employees report to each manager, a narrow span of control and a lengthy hierarchical structure will result—this is known as a tall organization. On the other hand, if many employees report to each manager, the result is a wide span of control, creating a flat organization. Because it is determined by so many factors, span of control is helpful in understanding organizational design and behaviors. One factor is organizational size; due to costs, large organizations tend to have a narrow span of control, while smaller organizations typically have a wider span of control. Required job skills must also be considered: tasks involving fewer skills will require less supervision, allowing a wider span of control. Complex tasks may need a narrower span of control, where supervisors can provide more individualized attention. Another factor is organizational culture; flexible workplaces typically have a wider span of control because the organization provides a more autonomous environment in which employees need little supervision. Finally, manager workload is a key factor. Managers should be able to plan departmental activities, train staff, and manage performance while being accountable for their own individual responsibilities.

Spans of control can be purposefully widened by giving workers more autonomy and holding them accountable to manage themselves. Standardizing the work processes of junior employees to avoid costly mistakes will also widen the span of control. As the span of control widens in an organization, the number of relationships among managers grows, too.

RISK MANAGEMENT AND BUSINESS CONTINUITY

Risk management includes ensuring regulatory compliance, protecting employee safety and security, mitigating and eliminating workplace hazards, planning an organization's security strategy, and more. All companies with employees must comply with all relevant federal and state employment laws. This section will discuss some aspects of security as well as business continuity in case of emergency. Workplace hazards and employee confidentiality are discussed in chapter 5.

Security

Just as a home needs to be secure from intruders, an organization also has SECURITY needs. A data breach, for example, can lead to key information being leaked to competitors and harm the organization financially. An intruder breaking in to the company's headquarters can steal important records, potentially resulting in financial or other losses. Protecting the physical security of the organization's employees, facilities, infrastructure, and resources is vital to its survival. An organization should carefully plan its security strategy.

Figure 1.3. Components of Organizational Security

1. Develop security policies and procedures that are well documented and accessible to all employees. This documentation shows the organization's commitment to security and clarifies procedures to management, which enforces security concerns on a day-to-day basis.

2. Maintain a physically secure environment. If the business is at risk of theft, robberies, violence, or other crimes, it is important to install surveillance, secure entries, metal detectors, and other devices to monitor the premises and prevent security breaches. The organization should also have policies and procedures regarding employees' handling of company equipment, including computers. The policies should clearly indicate what steps the employee should take when company property is lost or stolen, so that the organization can respond appropriately and mitigate the effects of that loss.

3. Restrict information only to those who need to know it. Employees should only have access to the files, records,

and information necessary to conduct their jobs. In particular, limit access to sensitive information only to those who need it in order to perform a certain function or who are in a position to make decisions related to that information. Additionally, the company should have a policy requiring employees to protect the confidentiality of any sensitive or proprietary information to which they have access.

4. Protect data from loss, theft, or intrusion. Viruses, malware, and cyber-attacks threaten an organization's technological infrastructure. The organization should install the appropriate firewalls, anti-virus software, and network monitoring software necessary to protect its infrastructure from attacks. Employees should be required to maintain strong computer and network passwords; these passwords should be changed regularly. The organization should have "acceptable use" policies restricting employees from accessing non-work related websites (to minimize inadvertent downloads that can be harmful to their computer or even the entire network); this can usually be achieved by installing web filtering software on the network.

5. Protect financial assets from loss or theft. If the company interacts with the general public and employees have access to certain cash reserves, protocols should be in place to monitor the flow of money and require employees to balance cash at the end of their shifts. The company should also protect any reserves it has on-site by using a safe, and it should limit the funds it keeps on the premises to only the amount necessary to conduct daily business.

6. Train employees on security practices and hold them accountable. Poor training often leads to security breaches, and thorough training conducted periodically will keep employees aware and invested in the security of the business.

Risk management includes being prepared for disasters like hurricanes, fires, terrorist attacks, and other catastrophic events. HR practitioners are valuable partners in **BUSINESS CONTINUITY** planning through the development of policies and procedures; furthermore, they manage employee aspects of business continuity, including staffing plans, medical emergencies, allocation of resources, and other concerns. The planning and execution of business continuity processes falls in four phases, as outlined in Figure 1.4.

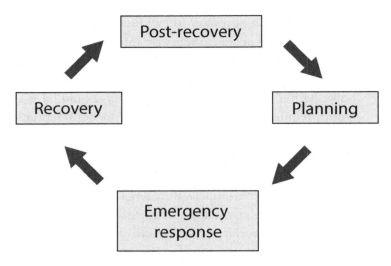

Figure 1.4. Phases of Business Continuity

Planning Phase

During the planning phase, HR practitioners help the organization develop clear goals, procedures, and expectations that are then communicated to employees. Typically, these policies are included in the employee handbook, and employees are trained and re-trained on a periodic basis. The policies and procedures should outline important information the employees need to know, including:

- how the business will continue operations in the event of disaster
- the employee's role in maintaining contact with the employer
- how employees should handle certain hazards such as fire or power outages
- how the organization will notify employees of changes to business operations or safety procedures during a disaster

Additionally, the business should develop a more detailed business continuity plan outlining asset recovery, employee mobilization, operations continuity, and compensation. The recovery plan should address all the logistics necessary to mitigate losses to the business, such as:

- Who is responsible for notifying authorities? How will first responders obtain access to the facilities?
- How will employees be evacuated? What will the company do to help employees find medical attention and safety if necessary?
- Where will employees work? Where will they stay? How will the company keep track of where employees are?
- How will employees be paid?

- What resources do they need to continue doing their jobs, and how will the company provide these resources?
- How will the company's data, files, and information be protected to prevent disaster and recover from disaster? Are backup copies maintained remotely?

HR professionals play a key role in ensuring that the organization is ready to handle disasters and manage employees' whereabouts, safety, and business operations. Employees should understand their roles in the recovery process and should be trained periodically.

Recovery

During the RECOVERY period the organization will need to adapt to operating differently for a period of time. For example, employees may need to work remotely, certain services or production of products may be put on hold, or hours of operation may change. The HR department plays a critical role during this phase by working with managers to deploy and track staff and resources to keep the business operational. HR may notify employees of their roles, hours, and expectations of work during the recovery period; HR may also hire temporary staff if needed. The department can also respond to employees' immediate concerns and notify management of problems. HR can help fulfill employees' immediate needs by deploying emergency food, shelter, cash, or goods if the employee is required to be away from home and the normal worksite. Additionally, if employees are ill or injured, HR can notify family members and keep them informed. Having these needs met will help able-bodied employees to keep the business running as smoothly as possible despite changes in conditions.

Post-Recovery

Once the recovery period has ended and the company is ready to resume operations, HR's role is to notify employees and help them transition back to normal operations. In the POST-RECOVERY period, if the surrounding area has been severely damaged, HR must respond to employees' needs for time off to find a new home, recover from injuries, or resolve personal and family matters. During this period, it is important for the organization to remain as flexible as possible with employees and recognize their efforts to balance their personal and work responsibilities. Recognizing employees for their resilience and dedication to helping the organization succeed will keep morale higher. If employees feel that their needs are respected and that they are appreciated by the organization, they are more likely to remain loyal to the organization.

HR plays an important role during the planning and execution of business continuity procedures. If these processes are overlooked, the long-term success of the business and the well-being of employees may be harmed. Involving HR, management, and employees in each step of the process and keeping communication open and clear will better position the organization to survive disaster and protect its employees and assets.

LEADERSHIP

Since the early twentieth century, several leadership theories have developed. A few major ones—trait theories, behavioral theories, contingency theories, power and influence theories, and transactional theories—are discussed in detail below.

Leadership Theories

The theory that leaders may be identified by shared certain personality traits and characteristic beliefs is TRAIT THEORY. Trait theory originally saw these qualities as innate; however, theorists today postulate that such leadership abilities can be learned and developed. According to trait theory, leadership qualities may include charisma, assertiveness, empathy, integrity, and problem-solving abilities.

Another theory, behavior theory, considers three leadership types based on a leader's behavior towards others. The social psychologist Kurt Lewin postulated three styles of leadership based on behavior theory:

1. **AUTOCRATIC LEADERSHIP**: leaders rarely, if ever, consult their subordinates, electing instead to make decisions and plan courses of action themselves. Autocratic leadership fits situations when decisions must be made quickly.

2. **DEMOCRATIC LEADERSHIP**: leaders both guide the team and consult it before making decisions. Democratic leadership helps maintain a harmonious team atmosphere but can pose a problem if team members' ideas conflict.

3. **LAISSEZ-FAIRE LEADERSHIP**: leaders take a "hands off" approach, allowing team members to make decisions independently. Laissez-faire leadership benefits skilled, motivated teams requiring minimal supervision; oversight is only needed to help the team maintain focus.

A good manager is adaptable and applies the appropriate style, or a combination of them, to the work situation they face. CONTINGENCY THEORIES address the best style for the circumstance. According to the Hersey-Blanchard Situational Leadership Theory, leadership style should align with individual team members' maturity levels. Another example, House's Path-Goal Theory, states that leadership should depend on the team members' needs, the task at hand, and the environment where they are working.

POWER AND INFLUENCE THEORIES address leaders' use of those qualities to accomplish tasks. French and Raven's Five Forms of Power, identified by John French and Bertram Raven, include *legitimate*, *reward*, and *coercive* (positional power), and *expert* and *referent* (personal power). French and Raven found that personal power is most effective: referent power, or charisma, attracts people, and expert power builds trust—the leader is understood to be an expert.

Finally, TRANSACTIONAL LEADERSHIP, assumes that people are motivated by rewards for accomplishments. Therefore, this approach focuses on designing tasks and reward structures. In the transaction, the organization pays team members in exchange for completing a task or job. The leader will penalize team members whose work does not meet an appropriate standard. This approach is used in most organizations to get things done, despite the fact that it does not focus on the human aspects of leadership, such as developing relationships.

Expectancy theory states that people are motivated by rewards.

Other Leadership Styles

There are other leadership styles outside the frameworks previously mentioned, but they are still relevant in the workplace.

In BUREAUCRATIC LEADERSHIP, leaders follow rules closely and expect the same of their team members. This style is effective when working in dangerous conditions (e.g., operating heavy machinery, working with hazardous substances), when working directly with money, or when performing routine tasks. This style is much less effective in teams that require flexibility, creativity, or innovation.

A CHARISMATIC LEADERSHIP style seeks to inspire and motivate team members. However, leaders who rely on charisma often focus on themselves and their own ambitions rather than the organization as a whole. Charismatic leaders may seem infallible, which can damage the organization if significant, inappropriate decisions are made.

A SERVANT LEADER leads by meeting the needs of the team. Servant leaders lead by example and with integrity; they often show great generosity. This approach can foster a positive culture and high morale on the team. Servant leadership requires time and dedication and may not be compatible with more authoritarian, rigid types of leadership.

TRANSFORMATIONAL LEADERS expect individuals to meet their potential; they also take personal responsibility for their own actions. Transformational leaders are inspirational; they set clear goals and are able to resolve conflict. This form of leadership encourages high productivity and engagement. According to researcher Bernard M. Bass, they gain the trust, respect, and admiration of others.

Clearly, leadership is not a "one size fits all" concept; instead, leaders must adapt their approach to fit a particular situation. It is important for leaders to develop a thorough understanding of various leadership frameworks and styles in order to adapt to changing situations.

HR FUNCTIONS AND CONCEPTS

Human resource management describes the activities essential to managing an organization's employees, or its human capital. HR professionals oversee compensation and benefits, training and development, recruitment and hiring, strategic management, and other functions. The objective of HR departments is to recruit, retain, and motivate the best employees for the organization. To do so, they find ways to keep the company competitive in terms of its compensation, benefits, learning opportunities, career advancement, work-life balance, and other matters of importance to employees. At the same time, HR plays an important business role in the organization as it strategizes how to allocate staff appropriately, maintain regulatory compliance, and prevent risks. Aligning "people needs" with business needs is essential to the organization's viability and attractiveness in the marketplace.

HR functions or areas of expertise include recruitment, safety, employee relations, compensation and benefits, and compliance. HR practitioners may perform a combination of these or may specialize in one or a few. Some small businesses without a dedicated HR professional outsource these functions or join a professional employer organization in order to obtain the same benefits of an internal HR team.

Recruitment

Talent acquisition or recruitment in a human resources organization can be performed by internal recruiters, employment specialists, or HR generalists. As part of the overall recruitment process, they advertise and post jobs, source resumes, screen candidates, conduct first-round interviews, and coordinate with the hiring manager (or team). In larger organizations, recruiters' success is measured by the time taken to fill job openings (requisitions) and the number of positions filled. Recruitment can also be performed by external agencies or headhunters.

Safety

Workplace safety is essential, especially in industries in which workers operate heavy machinery, are exposed to chemicals or harmful substances, or work in otherwise dangerous places or situations. Employee safety is mandated through the federal OCCUPATIONAL SAFETY AND HEALTH ACT OF 1970. HR often facilitates or oversees safety training and maintains federally mandated logs for workplace injuries and fatalities that must be reported to the government. HR also manages workers' compensation issues for on-the-job injuries.

> In general, employers must keep a record of on-the-job illnesses, accidents, and injuries for up to five years.

Employee Relations

Employee relations strengthen the employer-employee relationship through measuring job satisfaction, maintaining employee engagement, and resolving workplace conflicts or grievances. Employee relations also include coaching employees and managers to handle difficult situations, investigating sexual harassment and discrimination claims, placing employees on performance improvement plans, and terminating employees. In a unionized work environment, labor relations functions include interacting with unions on issues like organizing campaigns, collective bargaining agreements, and union contracts. The employee and labor relations functions of HR may be combined and handled by one specialist or be entirely separate functions managed by two HR specialists with specific expertise in each area.

Compliance

Compliance with local, state, and federal labor laws is an essential HR function. Non-compliance can result in litigation and governmental complaints of unfair employment practices and unsafe working conditions, fines from the government, and overall dissatisfaction among employees. HR staff must be aware of federal, state, and local employment laws like the Fair Labor Standards Act, Title VII of the Civil Rights Act, the National Labor Relations Act, the Family and Medical Leave Act, and many more. To comply with these laws and maintain fairness in the organization, HR professionals help develop company policies and procedure manuals.

Compensation and Benefits

Like employee and labor relations, the compensation and benefits functions of HR often can be handled by one HR specialist with dual expertise. HR functions include setting compensation and evaluating competitive pay practices. A compensation and benefits specialist also may negotiate group health coverage rates with insurers and coordinate with the retirement savings fund administrator. Payroll may be a component of the compensation and benefits section of HR, but in many cases, employers outsource such administrative functions.

Training and Development

Employers must provide employees with the training and tools necessary for their success. New employees should receive an orientation to help them transition to the new organization and undergo adequate training for their job. Many HR departments also coordinate leadership training and ongoing professional development activities. Depending on the organization's financial resources, programs such as tuition assistance programs for college or advanced degrees may be offered as part of training and development.

HR Information Systems (HRIS) Professionals

HR INFORMATION SYSTEMS (HRIS) professionals maintain all personnel (and sometimes payroll) records, including employee names, addresses, emergency contacts, job and pay information, performance ratings, leaves of absence, benefit elections, and more. They also provide reports to leaders and managers to support personnel decisions or to monitor employee metrics such as turnover. HRIS functions may be managed by a HRIS specialist, a departmental assistant, HR generalist, or other specialist. (See *Technology and Management Systems* later in the chapter for more information on HRIS.)

HR Generalist vs. Specialist

HR professionals typically fall within one of two categories: generalist or specialist. **HR GENERALISTS**, also commonly called HR managers or **HR BUSINESS PARTNERS**, have a broad range of responsibilities in one or more of the functional areas of human resources. Larger organizations typically have **HR SPECIALISTS** with technical knowledge and skills in specific areas. There are different levels of generalists and specialists in an organization, depending on its size, budget, and other needs. Examples of specialist job titles can be found in the following table.

Table 1.3. Functional Areas of HR and Related Job Titles

FUNCTIONAL AREA	JOB TITLE EXAMPLES
Recruiting	Recruiter
	Recruiting Assistant or Recruiting Coordinator
	Talent Acquisition Specialist
	Staffing Manager
Training and Organizational Development	Learning and Organizational Development Manager
	Organizational Development Specialist
Compensation and Benefits	Compensation Analyst
	Benefits Specialist
	Total Rewards Manager

FUNCTIONAL AREA	JOB TITLE EXAMPLES
Employee and Labor Relations	Performance Manager Specialist
	Employee Relations Manager
	Labor Relations Manager
Safety	Risk Management Specialist
	Workers Compensation Specialist
HR Information Systems	HRIS Administrator
	HRIS Manager

The HR Business Partner Model

More recently, the tactical HR generalist role has transformed into a business partnership with senior leadership to develop and execute personnel strategies. Yet the administrative and tactical aspects of HR remain necessary for business operations. To be influential in the organization, HR business partners must position themselves as strategic advisors, champions for change, and operations managers.

Developing a strong understanding of the organization, its operations, and its external environment is essential for any HR business partner to become a strategic advisor to senior management. HR business partners must align themselves closely with the values of the organization and the vision of its leaders in order to be seen as valuable partners. To do this they must:

- develop in-depth knowledge about the business, including its operations, financials, and strategy
- build key relationships in the organization in order to influence the strategic agenda
- earn leaders' trust so that HR can contribute to business results
- be able to prioritize processes that will deliver the most benefits
- develop credibility through competence, honesty, and high standards
- champion HR solutions that will add to the bottom line today and for future needs
- act as a catalyst for continued business performance

As business partners, HR practitioners share the responsibility for the success of the business by executing HR strategies that lead to tangible results. HR business partners should be able to quantify HR's contribution to business performance and staff effectiveness in business operations. HR business partners ensure that duties are assigned to the people with the appropriate qualifications, design meaningful career paths to motivate employees, actively manage talent, create staffing and succession plans, and foster an open work environment where ideas are shared.

Policies and Procedures

Organizations must remain consistent as they grow, communicate with employees, and maintain compliance with federal and state laws. HUMAN RESOURCES POLICIES AND PROCEDURES ensure consistent message and administration throughout the organization. Furthermore, policies provide the organization with legal protection. Finally, they allow the organization to formalize its adherence to federal employment law like the Civil Rights Act of 1964 and other laws and regulations.

Moreover, policies must support managers in personnel issues, allowing them to respond to employee questions and complaints, and to independently address minor disciplinary infractions such as tardiness or sub-standard performance. Supervisors can remain authoritative and unbiased by referencing the policies if the employee questions how a situation is managed.

Policies and procedures help employees, too. By providing handbooks to employees, organizations empower employees with information, helping them better understand their own responsibilities and giving them access to information about work hours, paychecks, dress code, paid time off, harassment, and other employment-related issues. Furthermore, policies provide employees with guidance on whom to contact with concerns about their employment or other specific issues.

Finally, the manual serves as an example of how the organization administers policies consistently and fairly. In the event of litigation or a complaint regarding an employment action, policies provide protection to the organization. Human resource professionals should reference the policies when responding to questions and coach supervisors on the appropriate methods or procedures to document employee disciplinary problems. Policies and procedures should be reviewed periodically and updated to reflect any changes in federal and state laws, and changes in the work environment or organizational structure.

TECHNOLOGY AND MANAGEMENT SYSTEMS

The Human Resource Information System (HRIS), briefly discussed above, is a human resources management system or electronic platform for data entry, tracking, and reporting human resources information. The system maintains important static information about employees like addresses, social security numbers, tax withholding information, job and pay information, and benefit elections. The HRIS can typically produce static reports such as employee lists, as well as analytical reports like turnover, headcount, and other information useful for planning purposes. HRIS vendors package their systems with various capabilities, and some are more robust than others. Typically, a HRIS will provide the organization with:

- the ability to manage all employee information and records
- the ability to track applicants
- reporting capabilities on HR metrics
- the ability to post HR documents such as employee handbooks, procedures, and forms
- benefits administration
- integration with payroll or other HR management systems

The HRIS should provide data the company needs to track and analyze applicants, employees, and former employees. Some systems allow employees to update their own basic information (such as address changes or tax withholdings) and benefit enrollments. This frees HR staff to complete strategic functions rather than administrative data entry. Additionally, the data recorded can be used to make decisions regarding employment such as merit increases, promotions, and restructuring. Managers can also access information to effectively support the success of their direct reports.

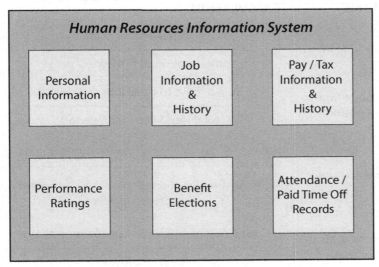

Figure 1.5. Information Collected in HRIS (Technology and Management Systems)

Other HR Management Systems

Other HR management systems may include an applicant tracking system (ATS), a program that automates the application and recruitment process. An ATS allows job seekers to find and apply for jobs on the company's website by electronically submitting an application with a resume and cover letter attached. Data is collected from internal applications through the ATS interface, located on the company website, or is sometimes extracted from applicants through job boards. On the employer's side, recruiters can post jobs, search through submitted applications, track candidate progress, and even communicate with applicants through the system. Despite the many capabilities of an ATS, its main function is to provide a central location and database to support the company's recruiting activities. The ATS helps recruiters maintain resumes and applications and stay compliant with federal and state employment and document retention laws.

A learning management system (LMS) is an application that supports an organization's training and development activities. It facilitates online training, tracks and reports on employee progress, and maintains learning aids. Corporate training departments use LMS applications to deliver online training, maintain electronic records, and automate employee registration in training programs.

HR Metrics

HR METRICS (measurements) show important trends and information regarding the organization's personnel. This information helps decision-makers improve the organization and meet employees' needs. HR practitioners can track and analyze several metrics.

Table 1.4. Common HR Metrics

METRIC	CALCULATION
Cost per hire	$$\frac{\text{recruitment costs}}{\text{compensation cost + benefits cost}}$$
Average time to fill a position	$$\frac{\text{sum of days to fill all jobs in a period}}{\text{total jobs filled in the period}}$$
Absence rate	$$\frac{\text{number of days absent in month for all employees}}{\text{average number of employees during a month} \times \text{number of workdays}}$$
Benefit costs per employee	$$\frac{\text{total cost of employee benefit or program}}{\text{total employees}}$$
Benefit utilization rate	$$\frac{\text{total number of employees utilizing a benefit}}{\text{total number of employees eligible to utilize a benefit}}$$
Average tenure	$$\frac{\text{total service for all active employees}}{\text{total number of active employees}}$$
Turnover (annual)	$$\frac{\text{number of employees terminating during a twelve-month period}}{\text{average number of employees during the same period}}$$
Turnover costs	total costs of separation + recruitment costs + lost productivity + training costs

There are more calculations that organizations can track and measure, depending on the organization's needs. When deciding which metrics to analyze and track, consider these factors:

- What metrics are important to organizational leaders and the strategic plan?

- What data must be obtained to calculate these metrics, and from what sources?

- How will data be analyzed, and against what sources will it be benchmarked?

- How can the analysis be presented for use in planning, development, and problem-solving?

MERGERS AND ACQUISITIONS

When a company undergoes a **MERGER** or **ACQUISITION**, the human resources department is a valuable partner in the process. HR helps the organization conduct its due diligence when evaluating a potential merger, plan a strategy for integrating employees of the other company, and manage the change process. Given the complex nature of mergers and acquisitions (M&A's), human resources can provide particular expertise in several areas.

Evaluating Company Culture

Every company has its own unique culture, and when two companies combine into one (through a merger or acquisition), employees may experience culture shock. When a company is considering a merger or acquisition, it should engage its human resources department in evaluating the culture of the other company and analyzing how well that company would integrate with the other. Organizational culture affects how employees work, what benefits they receive, the formality of the workplace, management methods, and shared work styles, attitudes, and values. HR uses the discovery process to determine this information; in this process, policies, procedures, communications, and other important documents are confidentially shared and evaluated. If there are significant differences between the two organizations, they should be thoroughly addressed prior to the merger or acquisition.

Identifying Compensation and Benefits Issues

During the due diligence process, the purchasing organization must also make a determination of whether the deal makes financial sense. Part of the financial data includes compensation and benefits. HR should review the compensation structures and benefit plans that the other company offers. It should identify whether the compensation structures and pay levels are compatible with that of the purchasing organization. It should also determine whether there are any inconsistencies between the benefit plans, such as a difference in premium costs, coverage levels, or funding of retirement plans (e.g., company match on a 401(k) plan).

Managing Change

Change is not easy for most people. When a merger or acquisition occurs, employees may experience anxiety about their job security or the future in general. HR can help alleviate some of this anxiety by communicating regularly with employees, being responsive to their questions, and being open to feedback. HR should monitor employee morale and identify any challenges, fears, or rumors that arise due to the M&A. HR can help alleviate uncertainty, dispel rumors, and make the transition smoother.

Organizational Design and Development

When one company merges with or acquires another, some functions or jobs may be consolidated due to redundancy. This process may happen quickly or over a longer period of time. HR plays an active role in restructuring the organization, identifying ways to work more efficiently and evaluating the impact of change. HR professionals are responsible for communicating changes to employees, revising job descriptions, handling difficult situations (such as layoffs or resistance to change), offering training as necessary, and motivating employees.

REVIEW

Main Ideas to Remember

- Strategic management is the ongoing process of creation, research, reassessment, and development. It is important to HR professionals because it affects how HR adds value to the organization through policies, procedures, and programs.

- All businesses operating in the United States are formally organized into one of these basic structures: sole proprietorships, partnerships, corporations, or limited liability companies (LLC).

- Common functions exist within almost every organization, including procurement/distribution, development, operations, marketing/sales, and customer service. General management (including accounting/finance and facilities), human resources, and information technology are core support functions.

- External forces such as the economy, consumer demand, laws and regulations, technology, and the labor force greatly affect the operations of an organization. Monitoring and adapting to these changes helps an organization remain strong.

- Like people, organizations have their own life cycles. They are "born" (established), they develop and mature, they decline, and sometimes they "die" (dissolve). The life cycle of a viable organization includes birth, youth, mid-life, and maturity.

- Through strategic planning, an organization determines its current status, direction over the next year (or longer), approach, and how it will measure its success. Strategic planning is important for an organization to focus on what is important for it to stay competitive.

- HR develops its own goals and action plans that align with the overarching goals of the organization. The strategic HR plan addresses the same questions used during the larger strategic planning process: where the function is now, where it is heading (within the organization), how the team will get there, and how they will know that they are there.

- As a result of the strategic planning process, an organization may decide that it needs to restructure itself in order to achieve its goals and remain competitive and viable in the marketplace by exploring or implementing structural changes like mergers or acquisitions, divestitures, reductions in force, growth in force, offshoring, or outsourcing.

- Ethical behavior begins at the highest levels of an organization. When the organization's directors, officers, and managers show their commitment to behaving ethically, employees are prone to follow their example. Companies develop codes of ethics and values statements, have whistleblower policies, and designate ethics officers to fulfill their commitment to ethical behavior.

- Organizational design is the alignment of people, processes, compensation, and metrics with the strategy of the organization such that the organization embodies its core values as specified in its vision statement. Leaders and managers must make decisions about how to group people together to perform their work effectively.

- Since the early twentieth century, several categories of leadership theories have developed: trait theories, behavioral theories, contingency theories, power and influence theories, and transactional theories, among others.

- The objective of HR departments is to recruit, retain, and motivate the best employees for the organization. To do so, they find ways to keep the company competitive in terms

- of its compensation, benefits, learning opportunities, career advancement, work-life balance, and other matters of importance to employees.

- HR generalists, also commonly called HR managers or HR business partners, have a broad range of responsibilities in one or more functional areas of human resources. Larger organizations typically have HR specialists with specific knowledge and skills.

- To be influential in the organization, HR business partners must position themselves as strategic advisors, champions for change, and operations managers. They must align themselves closely with the values of the organization and the visions of the leaders in order to be seen as valuable partners.

- As organizations grow, they must develop policies and procedures to maintain consistency throughout the organization, convey important information to employees, and comply with federal and state laws. Documented policies can also protect the organization in case of lawsuits or complaints.

- The Human Resource Information System (HRIS) is an electronic management system or platform for data entry, tracking, and reporting human resources information. It should provide information the company needs to track and analyze data about applicants, employees, and former employees.

- HR metrics (measurements) show important trends and information regarding the organization's personnel. This information helps decision-makers improve the organization and meet employees' needs. HR practitioners can track and analyze several metrics like turnover, time to hire, benefits utilization, and more.

- HR helps the organization conduct its due diligence when evaluating a potential merger, plan a strategy for integrating the employees of the other company, and manage the change process.

- All companies with employees must comply with federal and state employment laws. It is the responsibility of employers to understand all the laws that apply to their business in the locations in which they operate. Companies should develop sound, well-documented policies and train employees to ensure they can understand and follow them.

- Not only must companies comply with laws, but they must also understand and follow regulations, specific directives with the same force of law enacted by federal agencies to execute acts of Congress.

- Protecting the physical security of the organization's employees, facilities, infrastructure, and resources is vital to its survival. An organization should carefully plan its security strategy, which includes developing security policies, restricting information, protecting data and infrastructure, and maintaining a physically secure environment.

- HR practitioners are valuable partners in business continuity planning through the development of policies and procedures; furthermore, they manage employee aspects of business continuity, including staffing plans, medical emergencies, allocation of resources, and other concerns.

- The phases of business continuity are planning, emergency response, recovery, and post-recovery. Involving HR, management, and employees in each step of the process and keeping communication open and clear will better position the organization to survive disaster and protect its employees and assets.

Key Terms to Review

- acquisition
- behavioral theories of leadership
- bureaucratic leadership
- business continuity
- centralized decision making
- charismatic leadership
- code of conduct
- conflict of interest
- contingency theories of leadership
- core functions of an organization
- core values
- corporate governance
- corporation
- decentralized decision making
- divestiture
- division of labor
- divisional structure
- downsizing
- expansion in force
- external environment
- federal rulemaking process
- functional structure
- goals-based planning
- growth phases
- HR business partner
- HR generalist
- HR Information System (HRIS)
- HR metrics
- HR policies and procedures
- HR specialist
- human capital plan
- issues-based planning
- job specialization
- limited liability company
- matrix structure
- merger
- mission statement
- network structure
- Occupational Safety and Health Act of 1970
- offshoring
- organic planning
- organizational life cycle
- outsourcing
- partnership
- PEST analysis
- Porter's Five Forces
- post-recovery
- power and influence theories of leadership
- recovery
- reduction in force
- regulations
- regulatory compliance
- restructuring
- Sarbanes-Oxley Act
- Securities and Exchange Commission
- security
- servant leadership
- SMART goals
- sole proprietorship
- span of control
- statistical models
- strategic planning
- support functions of an organization
- SWOT analysis
- team structure
- trait theories of leadership
- transactional leadership
- transformational leadership
- vision statement
- whistleblower

2

TALENT PLANNING AND ACQUISITION

SECTION OVERVIEW

- What is the doctrine of equal employment opportunity?
- What laws prohibit discrimination in employment?
- What is sexual harassment, and what should the organization do about it?
- What reporting requirements do employers have with equal opportunity?
- What is affirmative action, and how does it affect an organization's employment practices?
- What is the OFCCP's role in enforcing affirmative action laws?
- How do HR practitioners analyze and document jobs?
- What are the basic components of a job description?
- How does HR plan for staffing needs throughout the year?
- What steps are necessary to find new employees?
- What is involved in onboarding employees?
- What is succession planning, and how does it help organizations in the long term?
- How do US immigration laws impact employers?

EQUAL EMPLOYMENT OPPORTUNITY

The Equal Employment Opportunity Commission

The doctrine of **EQUAL EMPLOYMENT OPPORTUNITY** prohibits discrimination against applicants and employees due to certain personal characteristics like race, color, sex, and other protected classifications. This doctrine ensures fair treatment in finding work, being paid, getting promoted, and opportunities for professional development. The **US EQUAL EMPLOYMENT OPPORTUNITY COMMISSION (EEOC)** enforces federal laws prohibiting employment discrimination[1].

Table 2.1. Federal Laws Prohibiting Discrimination in Employment

FEDERAL LAW	PROTECTIONS
Title VII of the Civil Rights Act of 1964[2]	Prohibits employment discrimination on the basis of one's race, color, religion, national origin, or sex. Employers must accommodate the sincerely held religious practices of applicants and employees unless doing so unreasonably hinders the business.
Pregnancy Discrimination Act[3]	Amends Title VII to prohibit discrimination against a woman because of pregnancy, childbirth, or a related medical condition.
Equal Pay Act of 1963[4]	Forbids paying different wages to men and women if they perform equal work in the workplace.
Age Discrimination in Employment Act of 1967 (ADEA)[5]	Prohibits discrimination against applicants or employees based on age (those forty years of age or older).
Title I of the Americans with Disabilities Act of 1990 (ADA)[6]	Prohibits employment-related discrimination against an otherwise qualified person due to a disability. Employers must accommodate physical or mental limitations of otherwise qualified applicants and employees with disabilities unless doing so unreasonably hinders the business. (According to the Rehabilitation Act of 1973, qualified employees or applicants with disabilities in the federal government may not be discriminated against.)
Genetic Information Non-discrimination Act of 2008 (GINA)[7]	Forbids discrimination due to genetic information—information about genetic tests, genetic tests of family members, or family medical history).

Discrimination in hiring, compensation, discipline, and termination—in all aspects of employment—is forbidden by the federal laws listed above. Furthermore, retaliation against an individual who reports or files a charge of discrimination, or who participates in an employment discrimination investigation or lawsuit, is against the law. Notices explaining federal anti-discrimination laws (prohibiting job discrimination based on race, color, religion, sex, national origin, age, disability, or genetic information) must be posted publicly in the workplace.

It is important to know that not all federal laws apply to all employers. Smaller employers (with less than a certain number of employees) may not be subject to non-discrimination laws. Additionally, states and localities also have enacted their own non-discrimination laws that certain employers must follow. Employers should monitor employment laws in all states in which they operate and determine how the laws apply to them.

Employers may not use employment policies and practices that disproportionately affect applicants or employees of a protected class in a negative manner, if those policies or practices are not related to the job and necessary for business operations. Employers may not use policies and practices that disproportionately affect applicants or employees forty years of age or older if those policies and practices are not based on a reasonable factor other than age. These adverse effects on protected classes are called DISPARATE IMPACT or DISPARATE TREATMENT.

Disparate treatment was established by the *McDonnell-Douglas Corp v. Green* case in 1973.

What Employers May Not Do

To comply with federal equal opportunity law, employers may not do the following in their employment practices:

- list job openings based on preference for a protected class
- recruit new employees in discriminatory manner based on race, color, national origin, sex, age, religion, or disability
- discriminate against an applicant or refuse to give an application to a person due to his or her race, color, national origin, sex, age, religion, or disability
- require pre-employment or post-employment examinations that may be inherently discriminatory against a person's race, color, national origin, sex, age, religion, or disability
- consider a person's race, color, national origin, sex, age, religion, or disability when making decisions about job referrals
- consider an employee's race, color, national origin, sex, age, religion, or disability in deciding job assignments and promotions
- discriminate in the way employees are paid, based on race, color, national origin, sex, age, religion, or disability
- consider an employee's race, color, national origin, sex, age, religion, or disability when taking a disciplinary action
- refuse a reasonable accommodation to a disabled employee, unless doing so would unreasonably hinder business operations

- refuse to accommodate an individual's sincerely held religious beliefs and attendance at religious services, unless doing so would cause a substantial burden to the business

Harassment

Laws prohibiting discrimination also prohibit harassment due to protected class. HARASSMENT may include derogatory or offensive comments or offensive verbal or physical conduct. Furthermore, it is illegal to harass someone who has reported or filed a charge of discrimination, or participated in an employment discrimination investigation or lawsuit.

SEXUAL HARASSMENT is a specific type of harassment including sexual conduct such as inappropriate sexual advances and demands for sexual favors. Minor isolated incidents are not against the law; however, if harassment is so pervasive that a hostile work environment develops, or if it results in the termination or demotion of a victim or other adverse employment decision, it is illegal.

Sexual harassment can include any behavior that may make an employee uncomfortable. Potential harassers may include not only the employee's supervisor, but also other managers, co-workers, clients, customers, or other workplace actors. Furthermore, inappropriate, unsolicited behavior or activities outside the workplace, if connected to the workplace (for example, between an employee and supervisor carpooling to work), may constitute sexual harassment. For these reasons, organizations typically develop strict policies against harassment with detailed procedures to report, investigate, and handle complaints.

Dress Code

It is lawful for employers to institute dress codes for employees, or those in certain job categories, with some exceptions. If a dress code conflicts with their religious beliefs, employees may request reasonable accommodations or modifications that would not impose undue hardship on business operations (the same rule applies to employees with disabilities who request a reasonable accommodation). Additionally, employers must not discriminate against employees' national origin: for example, if casual attire is permitted, certain kinds of ethnic attire must also be permitted.

Constructive Discharge/Forced Resignation

Under federal law, constructive discharge is also considered a discriminatory practice. CONSTRUCTIVE DISCHARGE is forced resignation, or when an employer creates such an intolerable workplace that a reasonable person would not be expected to work there.

EEO Reporting Requirements

Applicants or employees may file a **CHARGE OF DISCRIMINATION** if they believe they are the victim of discrimination in the workplace; in fact, in order to file a job discrimination lawsuit against their employer, all laws (except the Equal Pay Act) require them to file a Charge of Discrimination with the EEOC within a certain timeframe. However, Equal Employment Opportunity laws do not cover all employers; as a result, not all employees are protected by the EEOC. The EEOC's jurisdiction depends on the nature of the employer and work, the amount of employees, and the nature of the alleged discrimination. Filing an Equal Employment Opportunity (EEO) complaint does not automatically mean the company has committed any wrongdoing; instead, it is a formal allegation that an employer has discriminated against the complainant. The EEOC will launch an investigation, deciding if there is reasonable cause to believe that there has been discrimination.

Federal law requires employers to keep certain employment records, and whether a charge has been filed against a company, the EEOC gathers data from employers with over 100 employees in the private sector. The data is typically collected using a standardized **EEO-1 REPORT** and is used for a variety of purposes including enforcement of laws, self-assessment of equal employment opportunity by employers, and other federal research. Although a company's specific data remains confidential, aggregated data is available to the public.

AFFIRMATIVE ACTION PLANNING

AFFIRMATIVE ACTION is the policy of providing opportunities specifically for, and favoring members of, a disadvantaged minority group which has historically suffered discrimination. Affirmative action may include outreach to minority candidates, special training programs, and other positive steps to ensure a diverse workforce. Employers who are subject to affirmative action typically develop formalized affirmative action plans (AAP) and policies. These plans are reviewed annually and documentation is maintained to ensure compliance with federal rules and regulations[8].

Developing Affirmative Action Plans

An **AFFIRMATIVE ACTION PLAN** or program (AAP) is a tool employers develop and use to achieve their affirmative action goals. AAPs contain methods to measure and evaluate the composition of the workforce (i.e. the demographic makeup) of the organization and compare it to the relative composition of the available labor pools, or those in the same geographic region. An AAP also ensures equal employment opportunity by embedding this philosophy into the organization's employment practices, employment decisions, compensation programs, and performance management systems. Furthermore, AAPs include the practical steps an organization will take when people of certain classifications are underutilized.

An affirmative action plan describes the process a company undertakes to measure how effective its anti-discrimination efforts are. Employers typically audit and report on their affirmative action plans on an annual basis, measuring their progress. It is, however, prohibited for employers to establish racial quotas or to engage in preferential treatment of certain groups (including women and minorities).

Affirmative Action Requirements for Government Contractors and the OFCCP

Government contractors and subcontractors in the United States are obliged to take affirmative action under **Executive Order 11248; Section 503 of the Rehabilitation Act of 1973** and **Section 4212 of the Vietnam Era Veterans' Readjustment Assistance Act** when recruiting, hiring, and employing qualified minorities, women, people with disabilities, and covered veterans. According to these policies, federal contractors and subcontractors must ensure that applicants enjoy equal employment opportunity regardless of race, color, religion, sex, national origin, disability, or status as a Vietnam-era or special disabled veteran.

The **Office of Federal Contract Compliance Programs (OFCCP)**, part of the US Department of Labor, enforces affirmative action laws, regulations, and executive orders with government contractors. The OFCCP requires government contractors to practice affirmative action and non-discrimination in employment. The OFCCP routinely investigates contractors' employment practices and complaints of discrimination. Non-compliance with affirmative action or non-discrimination provisions violates federal contracts, and contractors may have their contracts suspended or terminated altogether; furthermore, non-compliant contractors may not be eligible for future government contracts.

Non-construction government contractors—those with fifty or more employees, and with contracts of fifty thousand dollars or more—must develop and carry out AAPs, according to **Executive Order 11246**, submitting them to the OFCCP as requested. These AAPs are intended to prevent under-utilization of women and minorities in the contractor's employment pool. Under-utilization is determined when the availability of women or minorities is unreasonably higher than their presence in the workforce for a certain job category. That availability is based on geography—the amount of qualified women or minorities in the geographical area where the worksite is located. Contractors must analyze the availability of qualified women and minorities and then establish goals to reduce or overcome under-utilization. Employers are expected to consider the candidacy of qualified women and minorities and to provide them with employment opportunities and advancement. However, employment decisions are to be made on a non-discriminatory basis. Finally, according to federal regulations, the OFCCP may not penalize contractors for not meeting goals.

The OFCCP takes a distinctive approach to construction contractors, as work in this industry is overwhelmingly seasonal and temporary. Here, the OFCCP itself, rather than the contractors, assigns affirmative action goals. These goals also detail the specific, mandatory steps for construction contractors to take to hire more minorities and women. For example, in 1980 the industry developed the goal of employing women for 6.9 percent of construction labor hours; this goal is still in effect today. These goals also detail the specific, mandatory steps for construction contractors to take to hire more minorities and women.

JOB DESCRIPTIONS AND JOB ANALYSIS

Every position within an organization should have a corresponding **JOB DESCRIPTION**, a document that accurately and completely describes the job. The job description provides an overview of the position's major responsibilities, identifying the knowledge, skills, and abilities needed to carry out those duties. It may also communicate the expected results of the position and explain how performance is evaluated. A job description, however, does not need to include every detail of how the work is performed. The following table lists the major components of a job description:

Table 2.2. Components of a Job Description

SECTION	PURPOSE	EXAMPLES
General information	basic position and pay information, which may also be tracked in the HR Information System (HRIS)	job title, position type (e.g., full time), FLSA status, pay grade, department, direct supervisor, direct reports, job code
Position purpose	a summary of the position's essential functions and its role in relation to the department or organizational unit	description of the role relation to the department or organization, estimated duration of position

	a list of duties and responsibilities (an essential function occupies a significant amount of the position's time and requires specialized skills to perform)	functions of the job— arranged by importance and percentage of time spent, essential tasks related to the accomplishment of an essential function
Essential job duties		
Minimum requirements	the knowledge, skills, and abilities needed to execute the main duties for which the position is responsible	education, length of experience, soft skills, technical skills, specific experience

Job Analysis

While a job description explains the duties for which a position is responsible and the skills required, the process of understanding a job and developing that description is JOB ANALYSIS. There are many ways that HR practitioners can perform a job analysis; typically this process involves interviews with the incumbent of a position, his or her manager, and those who work closely with the position. HR professionals use a combination of interviews, job shadowing, questionnaires, and sample job descriptions to develop job descriptions for the organization. However, it is important that the job description accurately reflect the essential duties and requirements of the job.

STAFF PLANNING AND THE RECRUITMENT PROCESS

STAFF PLANNING is a process by which an organization ensures it employs the right number of qualified people with particular skills to achieve organizational goals and objectives. Staffing plans require the cooperation of senior leadership, human resources, and management. The following list describes the various components of a staff planning program:

- job descriptions
- skills assessment of the current workforce (identifying gaps)
- turnover trends to predict how many people will leave an organization
- business trends examining both internal changes and the external factors

Once all relevant information has been collected, the human resources department (or staffing department in larger organizations) can forecast its staffing and recruitment needs. Typically, HR or staffing professionals work directly with business unit leads to interpret staffing metrics and forecast staffing data for the fiscal year.

During the planning process, HR and business unit leads will discuss the needs of the business unit, re-evaluate jobs and processes, and identify a staffing model that supports the goals of the business unit. In some cases, a job may be redesigned, combined with another job, or divided into two or more jobs. The needs of the business as well as the available budget will determine how jobs are structured and how many employees a particular business unit will have during the year.

Recruitment Process

Once the organization has developed a staffing plan, it will implement it throughout the year. As jobs become available (through turnover or growth), organizations will recruit candidates for these vacancies. The following is an overview of a typical **RECRUITMENT PROCESS**. Depending on the size, complexity, and culture of the organization, these steps may be more detailed or abbreviated.

Steps of the Recruitment Process:

1. Decide upon the recruitment process for the position: how many candidates will be identified, estimated timeline for filling the position, number of interviews, and composition of interviewing team.

2. Create or revise job descriptions to accurately reflect the essential functions and requirements of the job.

3. Develop a job ad based on the job description that includes information about the company, salary range, preferred requirements, and/or benefits.

4. Identify candidate sources and begin the search. Post job ads to job boards, social media, classified sections of newspapers, at universities and colleges, and other places where qualified candidates may be reached. Internal postings on a company intranet or bulletin board (for referrals) may be another method. Advertisements should include instructions for applying (e.g., an email address to submit resumes, or an online application system).

5. Pre-screen resumes and identify applicants who meet the qualifications of the job. Develop a short list of candidates for further consideration.

6. Conduct an initial **PHONE SCREEN** of shortlisted candidates and ask questions to understand their qualifications, gauge their interest, and evaluate their potential. Trim down the shortlist and invite the most qualified for an interview.

Employers must screen candidates thoroughly. Negligent hiring is a legal theory that makes employers liable for a harmful act if the employer knew about the employee's potential to cause harm.

7. Interview candidates (with interviewing team) and ask probing questions to further evaluate their qualifications and fit for the position. In some cases, a second or even third interview is conducted for the finalist(s).

8. Conduct PRE-EMPLOYMENT TESTS and BACKGROUND CHECKS of finalist(s) if necessary for the position or if required by the organization.

9. Make an offer of employment to the final candidate, including salary details, job role, responsibilities, benefits, start date, and other relevant information. In some cases, a verbal offer is made over the telephone and followed up with a written letter. Regardless, it is always a best practice to send a written offer with the terms of employment and have it signed by the candidate.

10. In some cases, the candidate may negotiate salary, benefits, perks, office location, and other factors. When an agreement has been made, it is also a best practice to update the written offer letter and have the candidate sign it.

Once the candidate has accepted the terms and is preparing to begin work, the organization should take steps to ensure that the new employee is transitioned and integrated into the organization properly.

Onboarding

Once new employees are hired, they typically go through onboarding or new hire training. **ONBOARDING** is the process of helping new hires integrate into their new work environment, learn their jobs, and transition into their roles. Done effectively, onboarding is a critical component of the overall recruitment process for the employer and the employee. Onboarding activities typically involve the following:

- a tour of the office or facility
- an overview of the organization—an explanation of the company's history, its products or services, and its mission, strategy and vision
- completion of required HR and payroll forms, as well as benefits enrollment (if applicable)
- training on the rules, culture, and procedures of the organization
- on-the-job training and job shadowing
- mandated training on safety, sexual harassment, non-discrimination, whistleblower, and other topics as required by law

While onboarding typically lasts only a few weeks—and, in some cases, may be as short as one day—a robust onboarding process can span one to two years. This lengthier onboarding process will monitor the employee's progress, provide mechanisms for ongoing feedback, and help the employee understand how he or she fits into the organization as a whole. For many organizations, a lengthy onboarding process is integrated into their overall performance management program.

Depending on the structure, size, and resources of the organization, onboarding programs may be simple or complex; however, they should at least address the logistics, training, and safety of the new employee. New employees should have ample time training on the job, and shadowing others if possible, in order to gain a total understanding of the product or service. With a holistic understanding of the organization and its operations, as well as a foundational knowledge of their own jobs, new employees are better positioned for long-term success.

SUCCESSION PLANNING

In order to remain viable and competitive, organizations need to ensure that they retain key talent to lead, manage, and carry out their mission and vision. As employees resign, retire, or otherwise turnover, it is important for the organization to plan so that key positions are constantly filled with the most qualified people.

SUCCESSION PLANNING is an organization's systematic approach to building a pool of future leaders to ensure leadership continuity. It develops potential successors in the leadership, identifies the best candidates for positions to meet future needs, and allocates resources to develop internal talent and create meaningful career paths.

Succession planning recognizes that some jobs are critical to the organization and therefore must be filled by the most qualified persons. Effectively done, succession planning is critical to mission success and sustains an effective process for recognizing, developing, and retaining top leadership talent.

The Succession Planning Process

1. **ALIGN STRATEGIC PLANNING WITH WORKFORCE PLANNING.** Identify the long-term vision and direction of the organization, and analyze future needs to develop and offer products and services. Use data to understand the current composition of the workforce and to make projections for future workforce needs.

2. **ANALYZE GAPS IN FUTURE WORKFORCE NEEDS.** Identify needs for competencies or skills, and determine talent

needed for future demands. Develop a business plan that is based on long-term talent needs rather than on specific positions.

3. **IDENTIFY TALENT POOLS OF CURRENT WORKFORCE AND CATEGORIZE TALENT BASED ON CAREER LEVEL, PATH, AND POTENTIAL.** Assess the competencies and skills of employees using formal appraisals and 360-degree feedback. Analyze external sources of future leadership as well.

4. **DEVELOP STRATEGIES FOR SUCCESSION,** including recruitment, relocation, and retention programs. Identify learning and development strategies, including job assignments, training programs, job shadowing, coaching and mentoring, and feedback mechanisms.

5. **IMPLEMENT SUCCESSION-PLANNING STRATEGIES.** Maintain commitment and involvement of senior leadership. Communicate activities with employees regularly and actively.

6. **MONITOR AND EVALUATE SUCCESSION-PLANNING EFFORTS.** Solicit and consider feedback from leadership as well as potential future leaders. Analyze employee satisfaction through surveys and informal feedback. Assess the responsiveness of the organization to change and future needs.[9]

Benefits of Succession Planning

Successful succession planning initiatives are based on the long-term needs of the business—they are an investment in the future. Senior leadership is invested in the process and helps to groom emerging leaders. Future leaders are also accountable for their own development. The pipeline of future leadership is based on anticipated needs. Careful analysis of the organization's workforce and needs guides the process, while the process itself creates meaningful career paths for employees, which can be a motivational tool. Finally, succession planning addresses workforce challenges like recruitment and retention.

IMMIGRATION ISSUES

Since the adoption of the **IMMIGRATION REFORM AND CONTROL ACT OF 1986 (IRCA)**[10], employers may not hire any persons not legally authorized to work in the United States and so must verify new employees' employment eligibility. However, like Title VII, IRCA forbids discrimination based on national origin; employers may not discriminate against applicants who look or sound foreign.

Immigration in the United States is overseen by the US Citizenship and Immigration Services (USCIS), part of the US Department of Homeland Security.

If an employer is aware than an applicant is not legally authorized for employment in the United States, or is an unauthorized alien, it is unlawful for the employer to hire him or her. An unauthorized alien does not have status as a Permanent Resident in the United States or is otherwise unauthorized to work in the country. Hiring US citizens ensures compliance with the law; so does hiring authorized aliens like permanent residents or aliens possessing **WORK VISAS** (authorization to work in the United States under certain conditions).

Table 2.3. Types of Temporary Work Visas[11]

VISA CATEGORY	GENERAL DESCRIPTION
H-1B	Person in Specialty Occupation. Requires a college degree or its equivalent.
H-2A	Temporary Agricultural Worker. For temporary or seasonal agricultural work. Limited to immigrants from designated countries.
H-2B	Temporary Non-agricultural Worker. For temporary or seasonal non-agricultural work. Limited to immigrants from designated countries.
L	Intracompany Transferee. To work at a particular entity or location of the current employer in a managerial or executive role, or in a position requiring specialized knowledge. Requires 1 year of continuous employment by current employer within the past 3 years.
O	Individual with Extraordinary Ability or Achievement. For immigrant workers with extraordinary ability or achievement in business, science, arts, athletics, education, and other categories. Must demonstrate national or international acclaim and continue to work in their field of expertise. This category also includes people providing essential services in support of a worker in this category.

Most foreign nationals, whether seeking temporary visitation or permanent residency, must obtain visas in order to enter the United States. Those foreign nationals entering the country for the purposes of work for a limited period of time require temporary worker visas. Prospective employers must file petitions with USCIS for all visa applications, and petitions must be approved before visas may be issued. Employing aliens without USCIS authorization is not compliant with federal law, and employers in violation of the law may be subject to severe penalties.

USCIS Form I-9

The US government issues **FORM I-9** to document a new employee's eligibility to work in the United States; it also certifies the employer's actions verifying that evidence. Form I-9 must be completed within the first three days of the employee's hire. However, if the employment is for less than three days, the form must be completed on the day of hire.

To validate an employee's ability to work, an employer's authorized representative must verify both the identity of the employee and the employee's status. Depending on the documentation, one or two documents may be required. Some documents, such as a US passport, prove both identity and authorization to work (categorized under List A of acceptable documents). Other documents (like a driver's license) prove identity but not authorization to work (List B of acceptable documents). Others such as certain Social Security cards, prove authorization to work but do not prove identity (List C). The instructions on the form indicate which documents are acceptable and which combination(s) of documents may be used to verify employment eligibility. According to the law, companies must keep documentation of I-9 verification for three years after the employee's hiring date or for one year after the employee's date of departure (whichever occurs later).

E-Verify

E-VERIFY is an internet-based system managed by the federal government that allows employers to verify a person's employment eligibility electronically. It is intended to supplement the completion of Form I-9. A company must participate in E-Verify if it is a certain type of federal contractor or otherwise required; otherwise, participation is voluntary. Employers may only use E-Verify after making a hiring decision; it is not lawful to use it for screening applicants or for other purposes not connected to verifying employment eligibility.

The E-Verify system will confirm an individual's eligibility to work in the United States. If the system reports a "tentative non-confirmation" (TNC) for a new hire, it means that that the system found possible problems in verifying the person's eligibility to work in the United States. In that situation, the employee may contest the TNC, during which time the employer may not take adverse actions against the employee. If it is determined that the employee is in fact not eligible to work in the United States, the employer may no longer continue to employ the individual.

REVIEW

Main Ideas to Remember

- The doctrine of Equal Employment Opportunity prohibits discrimination against applicants and employees due to certain personal characteristics like race, color, sex, and other protected classifications. This doctrine ensures fair treatment in finding work, being paid, getting promoted, and opportunities for professional development.

- Federal laws that prohibit employment discrimination include Title VII of the Civil Rights Act of 1964; the Pregnancy Discrimination Act; the Equal Pay Act of 1963; the Age Discrimination in Employment Act of 1967; Title I of the Americans with Disabilities Act of 1990; and the Genetic Information Non-discrimination Act of 2008. In addition, many states have individual non-discrimination laws.

- Harassment may include derogatory or offensive comments or offensive verbal or physical conduct. Furthermore, it is illegal to harass someone who has reported or filed a charge of discrimination, or participated in an employment discrimination investigation or lawsuit.

- Sexual harassment is a specific type of harassment including sexual conduct such as inappropriate sexual advances and demands for sexual favors. If harassment is so pervasive that a hostile work environment develops, or if it results in the termination or demotion of a victim or other adverse employment decision, it is illegal. Organizations typically develop strict policies against harassment with detailed procedures to report, investigate, and handle complaints.

- The Equal Opportunity Commission enforces federal laws prohibiting employment discrimination. It also collects workforce data from some employers (EEO-1 reports) for a variety of purposes including enforcement of laws, self-assessment of equal employment opportunity by employers, and other federal research.

- Affirmative action is the policy of providing opportunities specifically for, and favoring members of, a disadvantaged minority group which has historically suffered discrimination. Affirmative action may include outreach to minority candidates, special training programs, and other positive steps to ensure a diverse workforce. Employers who are subject to affirmative action typically develop formalized affirmative action plans and policies.

- An affirmative action plan or program (AAP) is a tool employers develop and use to achieve their affirmative action goals by measuring and evaluating the composition of the workforce of the organization and comparing it to the relative composition of the available labor pools. An AAP also ensures equal employment opportunity by embedding this philosophy into the organization's employment practices, employment decisions, compensation programs, and performance management systems.

- The US Department of Labor's Office of Federal Contract Compliance Programs (OFCCP) enforces the affirmative action laws, regulations, and executive orders with government contractors. As a condition of maintaining a contract with the federal government, the OFCCP requires a contractor to practice affirmative action and non-discrimination in employment.

- A job description provides an overview of the position's major responsibilities, identifying the knowledge, skills, and abilities needed to carry out those duties. This document may also communicate the expected results of the position and explain how performance is evaluated.

- The process of understanding a job and developing a job description is called job analysis. HR professionals use a combination of interviews, job shadowing, questionnaires, and sample job descriptions to develop job descriptions for the organization.

- Staff planning is a process by which an organization ensures it employs the right number of qualified people with particular skills to achieve organizational goals and objectives; this process requires the cooperation of senior leadership, human resources, and management. HR and business unit leads discuss the needs of the business unit, re-evaluate jobs and processes, and identify a staffing model that supports the goals of the business unit.

- As jobs become available, organizations will recruit candidates for these vacancies. The recruitment process includes posting the job, collecting and screening resumes, pre-interviewing candidates, interviewing candidates, administering pre-employment tests and background checks, and presenting offers of employment.

- Onboarding is the process of helping new hires integrate into their new work environment, learn their jobs, and transition into their roles. Done effectively, onboarding is a critical component of the overall recruitment process for the employer and the employee.

- Succession planning is a process by which an organization plans and grooms future leadership so that key positions are constantly filled with the most qualified people.

- According to the **IMMIGRATION REFORM AND CONTROL ACT OF 1986 (IRCA)**[12], employers may not hire any persons not legally authorized to work in the United States and so must verify new employees' employment eligibility using government-issued Form I-9, which documents a new employee's authorization to work in the United States.

- E-Verify is an internet-based system managed by the federal government that allows employers to verify a person's employment eligibility electronically. It supplements the completion of Form I-9.

Key Terms to Review

- affirmative action
- affirmative action plan (AAP)
- Age Discrimination in Employment Act of 1967
- background check
- Charge of Discrimination
- constructive discharge
- disparate impact
- Equal Employment Opportunity (EEO)
- EEO-1 Report
- Equal Employment Opportunity Commission (EEOC)
- Equal Pay Act of 1963
- E-Verify
- Executive Order 11246
- Executive Order 11248; Section 503 of the Rehabilitation Act of 1973
- Genetic Information Non-discrimination Act of 2008
- harassment
- Form I-9
- Immigration Reform and Control Act
- job analysis
- job description
- Office of Federal Contract Compliance Programs (OFCCP)
- onboarding
- phone screen
- pre-employment testing
- Pregnancy Discrimination Act
- reasonable accommodation
- recruitment process
- Section 4212 of the Vietnam Era Veterans' Readjustment Assistance Act
- sexual harassment
- staff planning
- succession planning
- Title I of the Americans with Disabilities Act
- Title VII of the Civil Rights Act of 1964
- work visas (and types)

3

TOTAL REWARDS
Compensation and Benefits

SECTION OVERVIEW

- What are the components of total rewards?
- Why are total rewards important?
- What is Maslow's hierarchy of needs, and what does it have to do with total rewards?
- What are the types of compensation an employee may receive?
- What are the different types of pay structures, and when are they used?
- What is the role of employee benefits?
- What benefits are required by law?
- What are the various types of health and welfare benefits offered to employees?
- What laws govern employee benefits and what protections do they offer?
- What is a retirement plan, and what are the different kinds of retirement plans?
- Why do employers offer work-life balance programs?
- Why are recognition programs important, and how do they benefit employees?
- What is professional development and how does it help employees?
- What is the role of the payroll function in an organization? How does it affect HR?
- What types of executive compensation are offered in organizations?
- What issues surround global compensation?

What are Total Rewards?

TOTAL REWARDS describe all the tools an employer uses to attract, motivate, and retain employees, including anything the employee perceives to be valuable as a result of working at the organization. There are five components of total rewards:

Figure 3.1. The Five Components of Total Rewards

Depending on available resources, employers offer these various programs or components as part of a total compensation package to employees. A competitive and appropriate compensation package is key to retaining and motivating employees, who in turn will deliver performance and results for the organization. In order to remain competitive, the organization should continually monitor the packages of its competitors and overall industry. Salary and benefit surveys are reliable sources of data through which the organization can determine its compensation and benefit programs.

COMPENSATION

Employee COMPENSATION refers to the cash compensation that employees receive in exchange for the work they perform. Typically, cash compensation consists of a wage or salary, and includes any commissions or bonuses. Cash compensation can be categorized as fixed pay, variable pay, or premium pay.

Types of Compensation

- FIXED PAY (OR BASE PAY) is nondiscretionary compensation that does not fluctuate based on performance or results. It is linked to the organization's pay philosophy and structure and to market conditions; examples include salary pay and hourly wage.

- VARIABLE PAY is compensation that changes directly with performance or results achieved. It is a payment

Other types of variable pay include piecework, gainsharing, and pay for performance.

based on a performance over a specified period of time and can be linked to either or both the employee's and employer's performance. Examples include commissions, bonuses, short-term incentives, stock options, performance-sharing incentives, and profit sharing.

- **PREMIUM PAY** is compensation that is tied to nontraditional work schedules, shifts, and skills; premium pay is provided in addition to fixed pay. Some examples of premium pay are shift differential pay, weekend/holiday pay, on-call pay, and skills-based pay.

Pay Structures

A company's **PAY PHILOSOPHY** or **COMPENSATION PHILOSOPHY** is simply its perspective on employee compensation. **PAY STRUCTURE** allows HR to carry out compensation philosophy fairly; it also indicates both how much value the organization places on a position and why employees are compensated at different rates.

There are two common types of pay structure, or administration of compensation: internal equity method and market pricing. According to the **INTERNAL EQUITY METHOD**, pay for a job is based on where that position is placed in the hierarchy of the organization, whereas **MARKET PRICING** determines pay as per the market rate. If a company's pay philosophy states that all staff should be paid at market rate, its pay philosophy is likely based on market pricing; on the other hand, a company that decides to pay some staff above market rate may pay according to the internal equity method. Finally, pay structure facilitates administration of incentive compensation, particularly for employees who have high levels of responsibility.

To establish pay structures and determine the appropriate pay levels for jobs, HR professionals typically conduct a structured **COMPENSATION ANALYSIS**.

Table 3.1. Compensation Analysis

1. Determine payroll budget.	Research merit increases and salary adjustments in the company and in the industry.
	Determine how many jobs need to be priced.
	Project upcoming payroll budgets to account for these adjustments.
2. Benchmark each job's value.	Use salary surveys to match the compensation of the internal job to an external job with similar duties. Compare with other jobs in the same industry or geographical location.
	Determine the benchmarked value based on the organization's compensation philosophy. For example, if the organization decides to pay "at market," the fiftieth percentile should be reviewed.

Table 3.1. Compensation Analysis (continued)

	Use internal equity method to create a series of grades or bands, with wide ranges at the top of the structure and narrower ranges at the bottom. Each grade is tied to a different level of responsibility within the company.
3. Create salary ranges and pay grades.	Pay grades should have a spread by which the employee can progress in his or her job. There should be a minimum and maximum amount for each pay grade. Typically, the midpoint of a given grade should be fifteen percent higher than that of the lower grade.
	Slot jobs into pay grades based on their market value and/or relative value in the organization.

Executive Compensation

To attract and retain the most qualified executive team, organizations sometimes offer a unique package of executive benefits and compensation for presidents, C-level executives, vice presidents, and senior directors. **EXECUTIVE COMPENSATION** differs from packages offered to lower-level employees. Executive compensation packages often include:

- base salary
- bonuses or performance incentives
- signing bonus for joining the organization
- stock options
- income protection in the event of a company sale or liquidation
- predetermined severance package for termination without cause
- additional executive-only benefits such additional insurance coverage
- company perquisites (perks)

As with any other compensation, executive compensation is negotiated between the potential executive and the employer. However, the structure or terms may be substantially different from the "regular" package offered to other employees, and it may be specifically customized for the executive (e.g., different structure from that offered to other executives). Typically, executive salary and benefits are documented in the form of an employment contract or agreement. This document outlines the terms of employment including the full spectrum of compensation, benefits, perks, performance incentives, and severance agreements. In contrast with an offer letter provided to a lower-level employee offer letter, executive compensation agreements are more detailed and contain a variety of benefits and perks not offered to other levels of employees.

BENEFITS

Employee benefits are important to the livelihood of employees and their families. The benefits that an organization offers to employees not only help the employees with their health, financial, and personal needs, but they also make a total compensation package competitive and rich. The benefits an employer offers may be a deciding factor to convince a talented individual to work at the organization.

EMPLOYEE BENEFITS fall into two categories: mandated benefits, or those that employers are legally required to provide, and those which an employer may choose to offer, either as a form of compensation or as a way to comply with a collective bargaining agreement. Unemployment insurance and worker's compensation are mandated benefits. Some optional benefits are retirement plans and, in some cases, forms of health insurance coverage.

Mandated Benefits

The following table provides an overview benefits that are MANDATED by law. (Certain health-related benefits are covered in more depth in *Health and Welfare Benefits*). Note that some states may require additional benefits for workers in those states[1].

Table 3.2. Mandated Benefits

MANDATED BENEFIT	PURPOSE
Social Security Taxes	Employers and employees must pay Social Security taxes at the same rate; these taxes are used to fund retirement income.
Unemployment Insurance	Eligible workers receive unemployment benefits provided that they become unemployed through no fault of their own; furthermore, they must meet other requirements for eligibility under state law. Unemployment insurance programs differ by state but follow federal guidelines.
Workers' Compensation Insurance	If an employee becomes injured or ill in connection with his or her job, the employer must provide workers' compensation benefits like payment for lost wages or payment of medical bills. Workers' Compensation Insurance coverage is available to employers through insurance carriers or their state's program; they may also carry it on a self-insured basis.

Table 3.2. Mandated Benefits (continued)

MANDATED BENEFIT	PURPOSE
Disability Insurance	In some states, companies must insure employees for loss of wages due to non-work-related illness or injury, providing some replacement for lost income during the period of disability.
Family and Medical Leave	Eligible employees may take up to twelve weeks of unpaid leave during a twelve-month period, under the Family and Medical Leave Act (FMLA), in order to 1. attend to the birth of and care of their child, or attend to the adoption of a child or placement of a child for foster care with the employee; or 2. care for an immediate family member with a serious health condition (a spouse, child or parent) or 3. care for the employee's own serious health condition. During their leave, employees must also retain their group health benefits by law.
Military Family Leave (FMLA)	The FMLA was amended in 2008 to provide protections specifically for military families. Eligible, covered employees receive up to twenty-six weeks of military caregiver leave to take care of injured family members and up to twelve weeks of qualifying exigency leave to tend to matters related to deployment. These leaves are also unpaid; however, the employee's must retain group health benefits during the leave.
Patient Protection and Affordable Care Act (PPACA)	Certain employers must provide affordable, minimum value health insurance to full-time employees and dependents under the PPACA.

Health and Welfare Benefits

HEALTH AND WELFARE BENEFITS are the most common discretionary benefits offered by employers. These benefits are typically offered in the form of a group health plan established or maintained by the employer (or union), and they provide medical care for participants (and often their dependents) directly or through insurance, reimbursement, or otherwise. The following are health and welfare benefits that employers may offer to their employees as part of their total compensation package:

- medical plan
- dental plan
- vision plan
- prescription drug plan

- flexible spending account (FSA)
- health reimbursement account (HRA)
- health savings account (HSA)
- life insurance
- accidental death and dismemberment insurance
- short- and long-term disability insurance

Employers may provide most welfare plans on a pre-tax basis; unless the employee is very highly compensated, he or she will not pay taxes on the plan. However, highly compensated or key employees may actually amass additional gross income unless the plan fulfills certain non-discrimination requirements according to the Internal Revenue Code.

With a Code Section 125 Plan or flexible benefits plan, also called a CAFETERIA PLAN, employees may reduce their compensation such that they qualify for pre-tax employer-provided benefits coverage. Employees select from at least two options of cash or qualified benefit plans. Pre-tax benefits available under cafeteria plans include health insurance, flexible spending accounts, group-term life insurance, and other voluntary supplemental benefits (like dental care). However, cafeteria plans must not discriminate against other employees to privilege highly compensated or key employees.

Employees may make pre-tax contributions from their earnings for qualified expenses specified in the cafeteria plan by using FLEXIBLE SPENDING ACCOUNTS (FSA). Qualified expenses are usually medical expenses but may also include dependent care or other expenses.

A HEALTH REIMBURSEMENT ACCOUNT (HRA) is an employer-funded account that employees may use to pay for certain medical expenses. This account may be used to pay for the participant's out-of-pocket, qualified medical expenses until insurance covers the expense or the funds are depleted.

Employees participating in high-deductible health plans (HDHP) may qualify for HEALTH SAVINGS ACCOUNTS (HSA), medical savings accounts to which contributions may be made on a pre-tax basis—they are not subject to federal income tax upon deposit. Funds are used to pay for the participant's out-of-pocket, qualified medical expenses (and those of his/her legal dependents).

There are a number of health- and welfare-related federal laws by which employers (as plan administrators and/or fiduciaries) and health plans must comply (some of these are also covered in *Mandated Benefits*):

- The EMPLOYEE RETIREMENT INCOME SECURITY ACT (ERISA) covers most private sector health plans. ERISA provides protections for participants and beneficiaries covered under employee benefit plans.

Plan administrators and fiduciaries are required to meet certain standards of conduct that are outlined in the law.

- The **CONSOLIDATED OMNIBUS BUDGET RECONCILIATION ACT (COBRA)** grants employees the right to keep the group health insurance (and pay the premium) that they would otherwise lose after they quit or lose their jobs, or reduce their work hours. Most people can retain their insurance coverage for up to eighteen months (and longer in some situations).

- The **HEALTH INSURANCE PORTABILITY AND ACCOUNTABILITY ACT OF 1996 (HIPAA)** provides opportunities for people to retain (or obtain) health insurance during qualifying events; it also protects the confidentiality and security of healthcare information and provides mechanisms to control administrative costs.

- The **PATIENT PROTECTION AND AFFORDABLE CARE ACT (PPACA)** mandates certain employers to offer affordable, minimum value health insurance to full-time employees and dependents, to communicate about health-care marketplaces to employees, and to provide a standardized summary of coverage to employees (among other requirements). It also requires insurers to cover pre-existing conditions and cover all applicants[2]. (Check with the US Department of Health and Human Services for the most current information about the PPACA.)

- The **PREGNANCY DISCRIMINATION ACT** requires certain health plans to provide the same level of coverage for pregnancy as for other conditions.

- The **MENTAL HEALTH PARITY ACT** requires that when a health plan covers mental health services, the annual or lifetime dollar limits, copays, and treatment limitations must be the same or higher than the limits for other medical benefits[3].

- The **AMERICANS WITH DISABILITIES ACT (ADA)**, among other protections, requires that disabled and non-disabled individuals must be provided the same benefits, premiums, deductibles, and limits under a given health plan.

- The **FAMILY AND MEDICAL LEAVE ACT (FMLA)**, among other protections, requires that an employer maintain health coverage for a qualified employee for the duration of FMLA leave.

- The **UNIFORMED SERVICES EMPLOYMENT AND REEMPLOYMENT RIGHTS ACT (USERRA)**, among other protections, allows employees to continue group health coverage while absent from work due to military service.

Retirement Benefits

In addition to health and welfare plans, many organizations also offer retirement plans to their employees. Retirement plans are savings plans that provide for a source of income after retirement, substituting for employment income, usually established by employers or unions, or other organizations. They fall under three types of categories: defined benefit plans, defined contribution plans, and profit-sharing plans.

- **DEFINED BENEFIT PLANS** are company-provided pension plans in which an employee's pension payments are calculated (defined) according to the employee's length of service with the company and their earnings prior to retirement.

- **DEFINED CONTRIBUTION PLANS** are retirement savings plans in which the employer, employee (or both) contributes on a regular basis (typically pre-tax assuming certain conditions are met). There is no guaranteed benefit. The employee accesses his or her account upon retirement.

- **PROFIT-SHARING PLANS** are typically offered in conjunction with a defined contribution plan; they allow the company to allocate profit to the employees' retirement accounts using a predetermined formula and vesting schedule.

Other Benefits

In addition to major health, welfare, and retirement benefits, companies typically complement their benefits with paid time off, paid holidays, sick leave, and bereavement leave. Companies may also offer voluntary benefits to employees, such as critical illness coverage, long-term care coverage, wellness programs, automotive insurance, home insurance, and other coverage at a group discount. Offering a complete package of benefits to suit the various needs of employees helps attract well-qualified talent to the organization, and can be used as a retention tool as well.

Work-Life Balance Programs

As business demands continue to increase in the global economy, high-performing employees risk burnout. To manage and limit burnout, organizations offer **WORK-LIFE BALANCE PROGRAMS** to help employees integrate work and family life through non-traditional work arrangements, counseling and support, and concierge services. Employee assistance programs (EAPs) provide independent, confidential, and free counseling and support services in mental health, family life, and financial, legal, and other issues.

Companies with greater resources may also offer dry cleaning, childcare, on-site fitness centers, and other perks to help employees stay balanced. Additionally, flexibility in scheduling or compressed workweeks, job sharing, and remote working can make it easier for employees to balance family needs while performing well at a minimal cost to the organization.

Recognition Programs

RECOGNITION PROGRAMS can have a significant impact on business performance and morale of employees. Some organizations have formal recognition programs with monetary rewards; others offer informal or low-cost recognition programs. Regardless of budget, successful recognition programs share the following characteristics:

1. They reward results or behaviors such as meeting sales targets, saving the company significant money, completing an important project, or otherwise affecting the business in a notably positive way.

2. They provide feedback that is immediate and frequent, providing positive reinforcement for positive behaviors; furthermore, they can be used as a motivational tool.

3. They offer opportunities for peer-to-peer recognition, creating a positive team dynamic, camaraderie, and strong working relationships.

4. Recognition is public and is embedded into the company's values. When employees are recognized publicly by leadership, they feel appreciated and essential to the company's success.

Figure 3.2. Maslow's Hierarchy of Needs

A culture of recognition is an important tool to retain good employees and motivate new ones. Moreover, when employees celebrate their successes together, synergy in the workplace improves.

Finally, recognition programs help meet basic psychological needs. Psychologist Abraham Maslow theorized that human beings have a series of needs (**Maslow's hierarchy of needs**). These range from the most basic (physical needs) to the most complex (self-actualization). Maslow's hierarchy of needs is depicted below showing the levels of needs each human being must satisfy to reach psychological fulfillment.

According to Maslow's theory, two of the most important psychological needs of humans are the need for appreciation and the need to belong. Organizations can meet these psychological needs through recognition programs. Having psychological needs met is an important element of an employee's decision to remain at an organization.

Professional Development Programs

Professional development refers to the acquisition of skills and knowledge, both for personal development and for career advancement. It can take the form of formalized training programs, external training opportunities, and financial assistance with work-related degree programs. Below are some examples of common **PROFESSIONAL DEVELOPMENT PROGRAMS** that companies offer to employees:

- training seminars and workshops (internal)
- external seminars and workshops
- tuition assistance for advanced (work-related) degrees
- reimbursement for certification exams and recertification fees
- mentoring
- career coaching

Professional development programs are key to a competitive total rewards package and are mutually beneficial to the employee and the employer. Employees acquire new skills and knowledge improving their work, advancing them in the organization, and increasing their competitiveness in the marketplace. (In some cases, professional development activities are required to maintain mandatory professional certifications.) Employers benefit with a smarter, more efficient workforce that can attain higher goals; employers may also benefit through reduced costs thanks to improved innovation and operational efficiency.

PAYROLL

PAYROLL departments manage the payments, tax withholdings, and deductions of employees. Payroll administrators manage the following processes to ensure the proper and timely compensation of employees:

- calculating time cards
- calculating salaries, wages, reimbursements, commissions, bonuses, overtime, and retroactive pay
- tracking and paying company-paid holidays, vacation time, and sick time
- handling paycheck deductions for taxes, wage garnishment, insurance, and retirement savings
- coordinating with the accounting and finance department to report all payments and deductions accurately

While human resources and payroll are considered two distinct functions, they often work hand-in-hand (and are sometimes combined in smaller organizations). For example, when HR initiates the hiring of an employee, payroll introduces the employee's information to the payroll system, collects and processes the employee's tax withholdings and deductions, and adds the employee onto the roster for paycheck processing.

Smaller organizations may outsource their payroll and/or human resources duties to THIRD-PARTY ADMINISTRATORS (TPA). A TPA can help the organization administer payroll, benefits, and HR records, often at a cost lower than hiring full-time staff. Other organizations, especially growing ones, may employ an internal staff member (such as an office manager) to act as a liaison between employees and TPAs to ensure that issues are appropriately addressed and administration is handled accurately and in a timely fashion. Even larger companies may outsource all or part of their payroll and/or HR functions if it is in the best interest of the organization's budget, operations, and long-term goals.

Organizations often include both human resources and payroll management in the strategic planning process to ensure that those processes are closely aligned with the strategic goals of the organization. For example, human resources leadership can develop the appropriate strategies to attract, hire, and retain the best employees for the company. Payroll, meanwhile, can develop strategies to streamline processes, ensure high accuracy in recordkeeping, and provide excellent service to employees. Both functions can work together to conduct or assist in internal audits to ensure the accuracy of employee records and employment practices such as paying employees.

GLOBAL COMPENSATION

Global Compensation

Designing, planning and managing employee compensation and benefits on a global basis can be challenging, especially when companies expand their operations into new regions while attempting to remain consistent with their total rewards philosophy. When offering compensation and benefits to international employees, companies need to be knowledgeable of the country or region's culture and regulations, which can have a direct impact on the types of compensation and benefit programs the company offers to employees in a particular location.

Centralized Approach to Global Compensation

When organizations centralize their approach to global compensation, they create a centralized compensation structure that provides guidelines for all positions in all locations, while maintaining a degree of flexibility to manage the unique needs and expectations of the workforce in various locations. A centralized system can provide tangible benefits to the organization, including simplified financial planning, increased transparency in compensation practices, consistency in the enforcement of compensation practices, and reduced administrative expenses.

While many companies take a centralized approach to their global compensation structure, these organizations also face ongoing challenges in implementing a centralized approach to compensation and benefits. Global companies must be able to manage variations in compensation structures due to economic factors, local customs that dictate what compensation and benefits are expected of a population, and holiday schedules that impact the organization's operations and compensation of employees. Furthermore, extreme differences in compensation and benefits between expatriate and local staff may negatively affect morale within the organization.

Common Issues with Global Compensation

In order to remain compliant and consistent with international customs, laws, and regulations, companies must handle many issues surrounding the compensation of their global workforce. Privacy and data regulations vary from country to country. Companies with employees in European Union countries must follow the *EU Data Protection Directive*, which sets restrictions on how personal information can be collected, stored and shared. The EU also restricts the sharing of data with countries that do not have rigorous security standards.

Another important issue is MAINTAINING PAY EQUITY. Base pay and traditional compensation structures vary from country to country. For example, in France, base pay can include vacation pay and overtime payments. Regional differences must be factored in to the overall compensation program, and they must be accounted for when analyzing internal pay equity.

Accounting for **COST OF LIVING** is a major matter of global compensation. The value of a US dollar in a given country affects the pay levels of employees in that country. For example, a position paying sixty thousand US dollars in the United States may pay eleven thousand US dollars in India due to the difference in cost of living. Finally, managing cultural differences is essential in effective global compensation. Appropriate communication with employees (especially with respect to their compensation and benefits) must be handled in accordance with the country's customs.

As organizations expand into international markets (or new countries), they must be prepared to address employee compensation appropriately. As mentioned above, this process is complex and requires knowledge of local laws, customs, and other factors. Companies should develop processes that align with their strategic plan, finances, and operations, while maintaining some flexibility to address differences. In some cases, the organization may decide to outsource its administrative payroll and HR functions for international employees in order to better manage the costs of operating abroad.

REVIEW

Main Ideas to Remember

- Total rewards describe all the tools an employer uses to attract, motivate, and retain employees. A total rewards package typically includes compensation, benefits, work-life programs, recognition programs, and professional development.

- Employee compensation refers to the cash compensation that employees receive in exchange for the work they perform. Typically, cash compensation consists of a wage or salary, and includes any commissions or bonuses.

- Compensation can be categorized as fixed pay (base pay), variable pay (incentives/commissions), or premium pay (holiday/on-call/shift differential).

- A company's **PAY PHILOSOPHY** or **COMPENSATION PHILOSOPHY** is simply its perspective on employee compensation. Pay structure allows HR to carry out compensation philosophy fairly; it also indicates both how much value the organization places on a position and why employees are compensated at different rates. There are two common types of pay structure, or administration of compensation: internal equity method and market pricing.

- To establish pay structures, HR conducts a process called compensation analysis, in which it analyzes its current payroll budget and trends; benchmarks a job's value using external data sources; determines the value of a job based on data and the organization's compensation philosophy; and creates salary ranges and pay grades.

- The benefits that an organization offers to employees not only help the employees with their health, financial, and personal needs, but they can also make a total compensation package competitive and rich.

- Employers are required by law to provide certain benefits to employees, including unemployment insurance, workers' compensation insurance, disability insurance, family and medical leave, and family military leave (depending on an organization's size). The Affordable Care Act requires employers of certain sizes to provide health insurance to full-time employees.

- Health and welfare benefits are the most common discretionary benefits offered by employers. These benefits are typically offered in the form of a group health plan established or maintained by the employer (or union), and they provide medical care for participants (and often their dependents) directly or through insurance, reimbursement, or otherwise.

- With a Code Section 125 Plan or flexible benefits plan, also called a **CAFETERIA PLAN**, employees may reduce their compensation such that they qualify for pre-tax employer-provided benefits coverage.

- The **EMPLOYEE RETIREMENT INCOME SECURITY ACT (ERISA)** provides protections for participants and beneficiaries covered under employee benefit plans. Plan administrators and fiduciaries are required to meet certain standards of conduct that are outlined in the law.

- The Consolidated Omnibus Budget Reconciliation Act (COBRA) grants employees the right to keep the group health insurance (and pay the premium) that they would otherwise lose after they quit or lose their jobs, or reduce their work hours. Most people can retain their insurance coverage for up to eighteen months (and longer in some situations).

- The Health Insurance Portability and Accountability Act of 1996 (HIPAA) provides opportunities for people to retain (or obtain) health insurance during qualifying events; protects the confidentiality and security of healthcare information; and provides mechanisms to control administrative costs.

- The Americans with Disabilities Act requires that disabled and non-disabled individuals must be provided the same benefits, premiums, deductibles, and limits under a given health plan.

- The Family and Medical Leave Act (FMLA) allows eligible employees to take up to twelve weeks of unpaid leave to 1) attend to the birth of and care of their child, or attend to the adoption of a child or placement of a child for foster care with the employee; or 2) care for an immediate family member with a serious health condition (a spouse, child or parent) or 3) care for the employee's own serious health condition.

- Retirement plans are savings plans that provide for a source of income after retirement, substituting for employment income, usually established by employers or unions, or other organizations. They fall under three types of categories: defined benefit plans, defined contribution plans, and profit-sharing plans.

- In addition to major health/welfare and retirement benefits, companies typically complement their benefits with paid time off, paid holidays, sick leave, and bereavement leave. Companies may also offer voluntary benefits to employees, such as critical illness coverage, long-term care coverage, wellness programs, automotive insurance, home insurance, and other coverage at a group discount.

- To manage and limit burnout, organizations offer work-life balance programs to help employees integrate work and family life through non-traditional work arrangements, counseling and support, and concierge services. Employee assistance programs provide independent, confidential, and free counseling and support services in mental health, family life, and financial, legal, and other issues.

- A culture of recognition is an important tool to retain good employees and motivate new ones. Moreover, when employees celebrate their successes together, synergy in the workplace improves.

- Professional development refers to the acquisition of skills and knowledge, both for personal development and for career advancement. It can take the form of formalized training programs, external training opportunities, and financial assistance with work-related degree programs.

- Payroll departments manage the payments, tax withholdings, and deductions of employees. Payroll administrators manage the following processes to ensure the proper and timely compensation of employees: calculating wages, reimbursements, deductions, and wage garnishments; tracking company-paid holidays, vacation, and sick time; calculating time cards; and coordinating data with the accounting and finance department.

- Executive compensation differs from the packages offered to lower-level employees. Executive compensation packages include base salary, bonuses or incentives, stock options, income protection, severance, and exclusive insurance coverage.

- When offering compensation and benefits to international employees, companies need to be knowledgeable of the country or region's culture and regulations, which can have a direct impact on the types of compensation and benefit programs the company can offer to employees in a particular location.

- When organizations centralize their approach to global compensation, they create a centralized compensation structure that provides guidelines for all positions in all locations, while maintaining a degree of flexibility to manage the unique needs and expectations of the workforce in various locations.

Key Terms to Review

- Americans with Disabilities Act (ADA)
- cafeteria plan
- COBRA
- compensation
- compensation analysis
- cost of living
- defined benefit plan
- defined contribution plan
- disability insurance
- employee benefits
- ERISA
- executive compensation
- Family and Medical Leave Act (FMLA)
- fixed pay
- Flexible Spending Account (FSA)
- health and welfare benefits
- Health Reimbursement Account (HRA)
- Health Savings Account (HSA)
- HIPAA
- internal equity method
- mandated benefits
- market pricing
- Maslow's hierarchy of needs
- Mental Health Parity Act
- Military Family Leave
- Patient Protection and Affordable Care Act (PPACA)
- pay equity
- pay structures
- payroll
- Pregnancy Discrimination Act
- premium pay
- professional development program
- profit sharing
- recognition program
- retirement plan
- Social Security
- third-party administrator (TPA)
- total rewards
- unemployment insurance
- USERRA
- variable pay
- worker's compensation insurance
- work-life balance program

4

LEARNING AND DEVELOPMENT

SECTION OVERVIEW

- What is the importance of employee communications?
- What forms of communication do organizations use?
- What are the various ways employees can learn new concepts?
- Why are training programs important?
- What training techniques can be used on employees?
- Why is feedback important? What types of feedback to managers give to employees?
- How do managers evaluate performance?
- What is the purpose of a performance appraisal, and how does it help employees as well as the organization?

EMPLOYEE COMMUNICATIONS

An organization uses EMPLOYEE COMMUNICATIONS to share knowledge with and obtain feedback from employees. The MEDIUM, manner, tone, and frequency of communications with employees affect employee motivation and organizational success. When people have regular and open access to information, can ask questions, and can provide feedback, they can more easily align themselves with the goals, strategies, and objectives of the organization, department, or team. Employee communications can be organization-wide (macro level) or employee-specific (micro level). They can take many forms including:

- announcement of new product or service
- information about company-wide benefits and open enrollment

- disclosure of company quarterly earnings
- announcement of business changes
- formal and informal feedback
- invitation to company-wide events
- explanation of new processes

Using a combination of media to convey information throughout the organization can be effective for reaching employees in multiple locations, with different schedules, or even with different learning styles. Below are some examples of media used:

- email messages
- bulletin boards
- company intranet
- company newsletters
- company-wide halls
- team or department meetings
- conference calls
- one-on-one conversations
- training sessions

The messages should be tailored for the type of media as well as for the audience (i.e., the whole company or a specific group of employees). Open lines maintain transparency with employees and ensure that messages are conveyed to and understood by employees. Mechanisms for information to flow upward (from employees to leadership) are essential for free exchange between leadership and staff.

A company and its employees can benefit from effective employee communications in many ways:

- Roles in the organization are clarified and employees recognize how they contribute to the "bottom line" or mission.

- Employees better understand changes in the organization by asking questions and absorbing information to adapt to those changes. This reduces anxiety, which would lead to lower productivity or higher turnover among staff.

- Customer service is improved when employees fully appreciate the product or service, and understand what is expected of them in their roles.

- Leadership can gain valuable input from staff about products and services, operations, or other issues, helping them to advance the organization's mission.

- Consistent and open communications establishes trust and encourages loyalty to the organization. Being upfront and honest can dispel rumors and encourage employees to ask questions.

It is important for leadership to communicate information regularly to staff and to solicit feedback. When feedback is received, it is important for leadership to be responsive. Two-way communication will maintain a dialogue, reinforce trust, and generate new ideas. When undergoing change, companies should establish a communications plan to ensure that messages are fully understood by all key constituents.

TRAINING AND LEARNING

ADULT LEARNING STYLES refer to the method by which adults best absorb a new concept. Some people understand a message by seeing it; others most effectively absorb a message by hearing it, and still others learn by acting out a process or through another means. To effectively communicate with staff, organizational leadership and human resources must be cognizant of adult learning styles.

Types of Learning Styles

- visual (spatial)—learning through pictures, drawings, and images
- aural (auditory-musical)—learning through sound or music
- verbal (linguistic)—learning through words (verbal and writing)
- physical (kinesthetic)—learning through touch or movement
- logical (mathematical)—learning through logic or reasoning

While it is not always practical to tailor a message or concept to every learning style, organizations should strive to use a combination of methods and media that are appropriate for the particular message and the available resources.

Training Programs and Techniques

Employee training programs are important for educating staff, preparing them to perform a job, and helping them acquire valuable skills that are relevant to the job. In other words, training helps employees acquire the tools, strategies, and techniques necessary to be successful at their jobs. Training methods fall into two main categories: cognitive and behavioral.

COGNITIVE METHODS OF TRAINING are based on theoretical training that focuses on processes, guidelines, methods, and rules.

Information is provided either in verbal or written form and results in increased knowledge or change of mindset. Examples of cognitive-based training include:

- live demonstrations and tutorials
- lectures to provide information
- group discussions for process-based problem solving
- computer or web-based training

BEHAVIORAL METHODS OF TRAINING are interactive and intended to spark creative thinking. They focus on employee behaviors and problem-solving rather than processes. Examples of behavioral training include:

- role playing with open-ended problem solving
- behavior modeling to compare scenarios
- case studies with open discussion about outcomes
- group brainstorming to solve sample problems

Cognitive training can be useful for providing consistency; however it does not encourage creative thinking. Behavioral methods challenge trainees to develop their own solutions, but they do not offer uniformity. The organization should account for the advantages and disadvantages of each method and the desired outcome of training when determining which type of training to utilize. In addition, although these two methods of training are the most commonly used, other effective training methods include one-on-one coaching and mentoring, soft skills training, and formal and informal feedback.

Kirkpatrick's Four Levels of Learning Evaluation allow effective evaluation of training programs.

1. Reaction—satisfaction with training

2. Learning—degree to which participants' skills or knowledge increased due to training

3. Behavior—degree to which participants' behavior increased due to training

4. Results—results achieved due to training (improved productivity, quality of work, or other factors)

EMPLOYEE FEEDBACK AND PERFORMANCE APPRAISAL

Feedback is one of the most important duties of managers and is critical to an employee's success. HR practitioners have a key role in collaborating with management to ensure that feedback is timely, consistent, and impactful. Feedback can be formal (e.g. performance reviews, write-ups) or can be informal (e.g. conversations, meetings).

Informal Feedback

INFORMAL FEEDBACK is instant, in-the-moment advice that occurs outside the formal performance review (which occurs typically once a year). Examples of informal feedback include: praising an employee for accomplishing a goal, correcting a mistake, or providing **CONSTRUCTIVE CRITICISM**. Feedback should be specific, utilize data or examples, and immediate. Providing feedback can help good employees sustain their success, and coach poor or average employees in taking immediate steps to improve. Managers can and should provide feedback to employees in the situations that follow.

Situations for positive reinforcement:

- when an employee demonstrates improvement in a development area
- when an employee goes "above and beyond," or exceeds, his or her job responsibilities
- when an employee "pitches in," helping colleagues beyond the bounds of his or her job duties
- when an employee reaches an important goal or milestone
- when an employee sets a good example for others

Situations for constructive criticism:

- when an employee is not performing the job correctly and is making mistakes
- when an employee is being disruptive to the team or not following rules
- when an employee is not meeting the expectations of the job
- when an employee needs to develop a particular skill

Employees usually perform better when they receive timely and specific feedback from their managers. Sometimes employees are not aware that their performance is problematic; likewise, they may be unaware that they are exceeding expectations. Feedback provides them with specific information they need about the manager's expectations, so they can correct their behavior (when receiving constructive feedback) or continue on the same path (when receiving praise). When the employee's behavior changes (whether positively or negatively), it is important for the manager to follow up and give new feedback as necessary.

Performance Appraisals

In addition to informal feedback, formal feedback is an important way to support the success of the organization's workforce. The most common type of formal feedback is the **PERFORMANCE APPRAISAL**, which is a documented assessment of the employee's performance in a specific period of time (typically a year) that contributes to the employee's overall development.

According the Society for Human Resource Management (SHRM), performance appraisals complement the organization's strategic plan, which determines individual job tasks and requirements. The appraisal is based on results achieved by the employee in his or her job. It measures skills and accomplishments with reasonable accuracy and uniformity, often using a predetermined **RATING**

Ranking is a method used to compare employees' relative performance. A forced distribution method of rating employees ranks them in order of productivity.

SCALE, rubric, and criteria. The evaluation should be conducted using specific data, examples, and feedback from colleagues or customers. Done thoroughly, the appraisal identifies areas to improve performance and helps the employee to grow professionally.

Periodic reviews enable managers to stay aware of their employees' abilities, to set a clear path moving forward, and to help their teams work more effectively. Performance appraisals should recognize the employees' achievements, evaluate their progress, and identify ways to improve or expand their skills. If the manager has been providing ongoing and specific feedback during the year, the performance appraisal should not provide many surprises to the employee. In these cases the appraisal is a tool for documenting the employee's progress. Typically, the appraisal is signed by both the manager and employee to confirm receipt of the document and confirm the performance conversation.

Appraisals are also tools for managing organizational risk. Sometimes these documents are requested during litigation or hearings with governmental agencies (for unemployment or discrimination claims). Organizations that have thorough, timely, and relevant performance appraisals documented in the employee's file can respond to complaints more effectively. If an organization does not document performance appraisals, or carries out appraisals inconsistently, it places itself at risk. A licensed employment attorney can help employers understand their particular risk and respond to complaints if they arise.

REVIEW

Main Ideas to Remember

- An organization uses employee communications to share knowledge with and obtain feedback from employees. When people have regular and open access to information, can ask questions, and can provide feedback, they more easily align themselves with the goals, strategies, and objectives of the organization, department, or team.

- Using a combination of media to convey information throughout the organization can be effective for reaching employees in multiple locations, with different schedules, or even with different learning styles. The messages should be tailored for the type of media as well as for the audience (i.e., the whole company or a specific group of employees). Mechanisms for information to flow upward (from employees to leadership) are essential for free exchange between leadership and staff.

- Learning styles refer to the method by which people best absorb a new concept. Some people understand a message by seeing it; others most effectively absorb a message by hearing it, and still others learn by acting out a process or through another means.

- Adult learning styles may be visual, aural, verbal, physical, logical, other, or a combination. To effectively communicate with staff, organizational leadership and human resources must be cognizant of adult learning styles.

- Employee training programs are important for educating staff, preparing them to perform a job, and helping them acquire valuable skills that are relevant to the job. Training helps employees acquire the tools, strategies, and techniques necessary to be successful at their jobs.

- Training methods fall into two main categories: cognitive (process driven) and behavioral (interactive). Each has its own advantages and disadvantages, and is appropriate depending on the learning styles of employees.

- Informal feedback is instant, in-the-moment advice that occurs outside the formal performance review (which takes place typically once a year). Examples of informal feedback include praising an employee for accomplishing a goal, correcting a mistake, or providing constructive criticism.

- Employees usually perform better when they receive timely and specific feedback from their managers. Sometimes employees are not aware that their performance is problematic; likewise, they may be unaware that they are exceeding expectations. Feedback provides them with specific information they need about the manager's expectations, so they can correct their behavior (when receiving constructive feedback) or continue on the same path (when receiving praise).

- The most common type of formal feedback is the performance appraisal, which is a documented assessment of the employee's performance over a specific period of time (typically a year). This assessment contributes to the employee's overall development. Performance appraisals should recognize employees' achievement, evaluate their progress, and identify ways to improve or expand their skills.

Key Terms to Review

- adult learning styles
- behavioral method of training
- cognitive methods of training
- communications medium
- constructive criticism
- employee communications
- informal feedback
- performance appraisal
- rating scale

5

EMPLOYEE RELATIONS AND ENGAGEMENT

SECTION OVERVIEW

- What is the role of employee relations in an organization?
- What methods do managers use to maintain employee relations?
- What is the significance of organizational culture?
- With what major federal laws must employers comply?
- What special obligations or requirements do recipients of federal government contracts, grants, or aid have?
- What laws affect specific industries?
- What is the purpose of an employee handbook?
- What information is typically included in an employee handbook?
- What protections do union and non-union employees have?
- How has the National Labor Relations Act changed labor relations? How has the scope of the law changed over time?
- How does an employee complaint differ from a grievance? How is it similar? Why are both important to employees and management?
- What are the steps of progressive discipline?
- How are employee relations and labor relations handled in a global environment?

EMPLOYEE RELATIONS

EMPLOYEE RELATIONS is the maintenance of employer-employee relationships to ensure high productivity and morale. Effective employee relations improves employees' understanding of the organization's policies, procedures, and expectations. Employee relations handles conflict, poor behavior, and difficult situations; this field also identifies ways both to prevent and resolve these problems. Employee handbooks are an important tool for maintaining sound employee relations through the consistent and fair treatment of employees; they also provide clear, written expectations. Handbooks and written policies are a key method to document expectations and practices such as fair hiring and equal employment opportunity.

HR professionals perform employee relations when they advise managers on handling poor performance or employee misconduct. For example, when an employee violates a policy that is documented in the handbook, the manager or HR professional can reference that policy and enforce it equitably. In these situations, a manager may decide to coach the employee or take disciplinary actions appropriate to the situation. When an employee complains about work conditions or supervision, HR may actively investigate the situation, interview witnesses, and make recommendations for appropriate action. Management or HR may need to interpret a policy when situations are not expressly documented in that policy, and they may take action (or make recommendations for action) based on the facts and the applicability of the policy to the situation.

The employee's manager or department may have his or her own specific procedures and expectations that are typically aligned with those of the overall organization. When employees perform poorly or behave in an unacceptable manner, the manager will identify the issues, counsel the employee, and discuss a plan to correct the problem. When an employee files a complaint about his or her work conditions, management or HR will discuss the concerns, investigate if necessary, and collect key data to make an informed decision. In serious situations such as sexual harassment or discrimination, employees are typically reminded of their grievance and appeal rights, as well as any whistleblower protections. When these situations are handled, they are often documented in the employee's file or another record repository for future reference or required government reporting.

A major benefit of sound employee relations is the ability of the organization to maintain open, productive relationships between employees and management. By proactively identifying issues and being responsive to complaints or problems, organizations can thwart or diminish disruptive behavior. Managers who actively support employee relations and act as problem solvers are key to a successful partnership with HR. When employees are aware of their developmental needs and have the support and resources they need to improve, both the employees and the organization benefit.

ORGANIZATIONAL CULTURE

ORGANIZATIONAL CULTURE is the workplace environment fostered by both leadership and employees. It describes how people within the organization interact with one another, and it is affected by the experiences, personalities, values, beliefs, and principles of leadership and employees. Everyone within the organization contributes to the organizational culture in some way, and every organization has its own unique culture. Culture is often a reason why employees decide to remain at or leave an organization; it can also affect the organization's success.

An organization's culture affects its overall identity—the way that employees, clients, and the general public perceive it. For this reason, many organizations take great care to articulate and instill their values in everything they do; by developing a strong reputation, an organization attracts strong candidates for employment and reliable clients to purchase its products or services. A shared organizational culture also helps to keep the workforce cohesive, especially when many employees come from different backgrounds, geographies, and cultures. Employees who feel supported by a sense of cultural unity and values are more likely to communicate effectively, work more collaboratively, and experience less conflict in the workplace.

Organizational culture is also a motivational tool. When employees feel connected to the organization and understand the significance of their role in it, they are more likely to feel invested in the organization's success. When they feel they have a stake in the success of the organization, they are more likely to work harder to accomplish the organization's goals. Having clear expectations and objectives set by management can help each employee understand his or her roles and responsibilities. This strategic management, combined with a system of recognition and feedback, helps keep employees aligned with the objectives of the business unit and organization. Employees will perform at their personal best to earn recognition and appreciation from management, and the organization will benefit from greater productivity and cooperation.

LABOR LAWS

There are over 180 federal laws that apply to numerous employment contexts, including specific industries and sizes of companies; the US Department of Labor (DOL) administers and enforces these laws and the mandates and regulations that implement them. Employers are required to understand and comply with these laws as applicable[1]. (Some of the following laws are also discussed previously in *Total Rewards* and elsewhere in this study guide.)

Wages and Hours

According to the FAIR LABOR STANDARDS ACT (FLSA), most private and public employers must pay a minimum federal wage and overtime pay of one and one-half times the regular rate of pay, or time and a half. These standards apply to non-exempt employees, or covered employees, who usually are paid by the hour. Children under sixteen can only work certain hours, and children under eighteen cannot work in dangerous non-agricultural jobs.

Garnishment of Wages

Employee wage garnishments are regulated under the CONSUMER CREDIT PROTECTION ACT (CPCA).

Workplace Safety

The OCCUPATIONAL SAFETY AND HEALTH ACT regulates the safety and health of employees; it is administered by the Occupational Safety and Health Administration (OSHA), which may conduct inspections and investigations of those employers covered by the Act, who are responsible for ensuring a safe work environment for employees, in compliance with health and safety standards.

Health and Welfare

Certain employers must provide affordable, minimum value health insurance to full-time employees and dependents under the PATIENT PROTECTION AND AFFORDABLE CARE ACT (PPACA). Employers are required to communicate about health-care marketplaces to employees, and to provide a standardized summary of coverage to employees (among other requirements). It also requires insurers to cover pre-existing conditions and to cover all insurance applicants. (Check with the US Department of Health and Human Services for the most current information on the PPACA.)

The CONSOLIDATED OMNIBUS BUDGET RECONCILIATION ACT (COBRA) grants employees the right to keep the group health insurance (and pay the premium) that they would otherwise lose after they quit or lose their jobs, or reduce their work hours. Most people can retain their insurance coverage for up to eighteen months (and longer in some situations). The HEALTH INSURANCE PORTABILITY AND ACCOUNTABILITY ACT OF 1996 (HIPAA) provides opportunities for people to retain (or obtain) health insurance during qualifying events, protects the confidentiality and security of healthcare information, and provides mechanisms to control administrative costs.

Under the FAMILY AND MEDICAL LEAVE ACT (FMLA), eligible employees may take up to twelve weeks of unpaid leave during a twelve-month period, in order to—

1. attend to the birth of and care of their child, or attend to the adoption of a child or placement of a child for foster care with the employee; or

2. care for an immediate family member with a serious health condition (a spouse, child or parent) or

3. care for the employee's own serious health condition

The law also requires that the employee must retain his or her group health benefits during the leave. The FMLA was amended in 2008 to provide protections specifically for military families. Eligible, covered employees receive up to twenty-six weeks of military caregiver leave (to care for injured family members), and up to twelve weeks of qualifying exigency leave (to tend to matters related to deployment). These leaves are also unpaid; however, the employee's group health benefits must be maintained during the leave.

The **EMPLOYEE RETIREMENT INCOME SECURITY ACT (ERISA)** provides protections for participants and beneficiaries covered under employee benefit plans offering welfare or pension plans. ERISA preempts many state laws. Plan administrators and fiduciaries are required to meet certain standards of conduct, including reporting and disclosure requirements and levels of fiduciary responsibility. ERISA also mandates that certain employers protect certain kinds of retirement benefits through an insurance system, paying premiums to the PBGC, the Pension Benefit Guaranty Corporation of the federal government.

The *Prudent Person* rule applies to ERISA, meaning that trustees must administer retirement plans prudently. Administrators should act only in the interest of plan beneficiaries, focusing on the decision-making process of plan administration.

Uniformed Services Employment and Reemployment Rights Act

The **UNIFORMED SERVICES EMPLOYMENT AND REEMPLOYMENT RIGHTS ACT (USERRA)**, among other protections, allows certain employees the right to reemployment following an absence from work due to military service, including those serving in the reserves and the National Guard.

Employee Polygraph Protection Act

This Act allows polygraph tests in only a few circumstances; otherwise, employers are not permitted to use polygraphs on employees.

Whistleblower Protection

Many labor-related, public safety and environmental laws, usually enforced by OSHA, protect WHISTLEBLOWERS—employees who report violations of labor laws. OSHA may ensure that whistleblowers who face employer retaliation receive payment of back wages or job reinstatement.

Notification of Layoffs or Plant Closings

Mass layoffs or plant closings may be subject to the **Worker Adjustment and Retraining Notification Act (WARN)**. WARN requires that employees are given advance warning of layoffs or plant closings.

Special Requirements for Government Contractors

Specific labor laws apply to government contractors or employers receiving government grants.

- The Davis-Bacon Act requires government construction contractors to pay prevailing wages and benefits to their employees.

- The McNamara-O'Hara Service Contract Act establishes standards for service contractors providing various services to the federal government, such as minimum wage rates to be paid to employees.

- According to the Walsh-Healey Public Contracts Act, contractors that provide the federal government with goods and materials must pay their employees minimum wages and adhere to other work standards.

Government contractors are also required to comply with federal affirmative action and equal opportunity laws, executive orders, and regulations. The **Office of Federal Contract Compliance Programs (OFCCP)** administers and enforces these laws.

Industry-Specific Laws and Regulations

Several federal laws and regulations affect employers in the construction, agricultural, and mining industries.

- **OSHA** promulgates specific safety and health regulations for employers in the construction industry.

- Employing agricultural workers is regulated by the **Migrant and Seasonal Agricultural Worker Protection Act (MSPA)**.

- Agricultural workers are exempt from overtime premium pay according to the **Fair Labor Standards Act (FLSA)**; however, these workers must receive minimum wage when employed on larger farms. Children under sixteen may not work during school hours or under certain dangerous conditions.

- According to the **Federal Mine Safety and Health Act of 1977 (Mine Act)**, there are standards for safety, health, and training of miners; furthermore, employers face penalties for violations of these standards, and inspectors may close dangerous mines.

State Laws and Regulations

The laws and regulations mentioned in this section are prescribed by the federal government. Individual states (and sometimes localities) create and enforce their own laws related to the employment of workers. Employers should be aware of the employment laws in all states in which they conduct business and employment; the state's Department of Labor can be contacted for state-specific information about employment laws. Employment practices and policies should be consistent with all laws that affect the organization in order to remain compliant and avoid penalties.

COMPANY POLICIES AND HANDBOOKS

An **EMPLOYEE HANDBOOK**, also referred to as an employee manual, is a document of the organization's policies and procedures that affect all employees. It can provide both employment and practical information like company rules, performance expectations, and office operations. A written employee handbook provides employees with clear guidance, explains organizational expectations, and fosters a culture in which problems are addressed fairly and consistently. It also outlines the organization's legal obligations as an employer and employee rights.

Sections and Policies in Handbooks

- **GENERAL EMPLOYMENT INFORMATION**: An employee handbook should provide an overview of the business and its general employment policies, including employment eligibility, job classifications, employee records, probationary periods, performance reviews, termination procedures, company transfers and union information, if applicable.

- **ANTI-DISCRIMINATION POLICIES**: The handbook should contain information about the company's compliance with equal opportunity, anti-harassment, non-discrimination, and disability laws; it should also include procedures for complaints and grievances.

- **STANDARDS OF CONDUCT** clarify expectations of employee conduct, including dress code and workplace behavior.

- **CONFLICT OF INTEREST STATEMENTS** help protect the company's trade secrets and proprietary information.

- **PAYROLL PROCEDURES** outline pay schedules, timekeeping requirements, overtime pay, salary increases, bonuses, and deductions for taxes and benefit premiums.

- **WORK SCHEDULES:** The handbook should explain work hours and schedules, attendance policies, punctuality, and reporting absences.
- **SAFETY AND SECURITY:** This section explains an employee's rights and obligations in ensuring a safe and secure workplace; it provides instructions on reporting accidents, injuries, and safety hazards. It also provides guidance on securing files, computers, and other company resources.
- **USE OF COMPUTERS AND TECHNOLOGY:** This section explains the appropriate use of company-provided hardware and software, steps to keep data secure, and how to handle personal information. Typically, it reminds employees that the company owns the technology and may monitor and regulate its use.
- **EMPLOYEE BENEFITS:** This section outlines any benefit programs and eligibility requirements, including all benefits that are required by law.
- **TIME-OFF POLICIES:** This section explains employee entitlement to vacation time, sick time, paid holidays, family and medical leave, jury duty, military leave, and voting; policies and compliance with the law should be clearly documented.

Many handbooks also contain specific language that invokes the doctrine of EMPLOYMENT-AT-WILL. An employment-at-will statement specifies that an employee or employer may terminate the employment relationship, with or without reason, and with or without notice. In an at-will employment situation (which is the case in many states), there is no expectation of employment either indefinitely or for a specified duration.

New employees are typically required to sign an acknowledgement form stating they have read and understand the information contained in the handbook. From time to time, the company may need to update the handbook to reflect new policies, practices, and laws. Revisions should be communicated and distributed to employees and may require a new signed acknowledgment. Additionally, there may be different versions of the employee handbook for certain business units, subsidiaries, or locations. It is important to ensure that all versions are kept up to date.

Handbooks can be a useful tool in situations when corrective action needs to be taken with an employee, including termination of employment. When disciplining or terminating employees, it is helpful to refer to the specific policy or policies being violated. Doing so not only makes it clear to the employee that corrective action has been taken for an objective reason (e.g. violating an established policy), but it also provides a reference enabling the company to better defend itself in litigation or complaints to governmental agencies. For this reason, a qualified employment attorney should review the company's handbook for compliance with the law and provide counsel as needed.

LABOR RELATIONS

The term **LABOR RELATIONS** describes the interaction between employers and employees, typically in a unionized environment. (However, in some cases it applies to non-union workers as well.) Labor relations also examine how employees are affected by economic factors like globalization and recession and strive to minimize their negative impact on the workforce. When labor relations are strong at an organization, management works effectively with employee representatives (typically labor unions) to solve problems in the interests of both the employees and the organization. For example, if the cost of materials rises substantially and threatens mass layoffs, the labor relations process could find ways to cut costs elsewhere, adapt to the changes, and innovate new, sustainable products or business strategies, thereby protecting jobs.

Labor relations are regulated by the US government, which provides guidance on the treatment of employees. A major law governing labor relations in the United States is the **NATIONAL LABOR RELATIONS ACT OF 1935** (also called the **WAGNER ACT**), which is enforced by the National Labor Relations Board. Thanks to the Act, private-sector workers can strike, bargain as a union, and protest the conditions of their employment. (The Act does not apply to management, governmental employees, independent contractors, and certain other employees as outlined in the statute.) Employees covered by the Wagner Act are granted certain rights to join together to improve their wages and working conditions, with or without a union. This means that although a union may not be present in an organization, employees at that organization still have the right to discuss the conditions of their employment and take action as a group.

The NLRA also protects employees who are not represented by a union but are engaged in concerted activity. Two or more employees acting for their mutual protection or benefit in response to their employment conditions is **CONCERTED ACTIVITY** and can range from actions like a group of employees meeting with a manager to ask for a wage increase to two employees discussing concerns about the workplace. If one employee acts on behalf of a greater group or attempts to coordinate a group or an action, he or she is also engaging in concerted activity.

The **TAFT-HARTLEY ACT** of 1947 weakened the NLRA by outlawing closed shops, secondary boycotts, and jurisdictional

UNION ACTIVITY
Under the National Labor Relations Act, employees have the right to attempt to form a union where one does not currently exist, and to decertify a union that employees no longer support. In exchange for membership dues, the union represents employees on matters related to their pay, benefits, and workplace conditions. The union will assist employees when they file complaints or grievances, or when an employer is not abiding by a collective bargaining agreement. Employers are prohibited by federal law from retaliating against employees who form a union or who engage in protected activity covered under the NLRA.

strikes. Taft-Hartley allowed states to pass RIGHT-TO-WORK LAWS and other anti-union legislation; the Act also facilitated decertifying unions. Unions would have to file documentation with the US DOL in order to obtain services from the National Labor Relations Board; management would not be eligible for union protection; and neither employers nor unions could contribute funds from their treasuries to candidates running for office.

Labor relations includes other legislation beyond the National Labor Relations Act and Taft-Hartley. Laws enforcing state and federal minimum wages, danger pay, fair-practice rules, and wage theft laws were all passed due to influence from organized labor.

Table 5.1. Labor Relations Vocabulary

Agency Shop	a union security clause that requires all union members and non-union employees to pay a service fee (similar to dues)
Arbitration	Arbitration is the referral of disputes to an impartial third party (an arbitrator, as opposed to court). The arbitrator's decision is typically final and binding.
Bargaining Unit	a group of employees who bargain collectively with their employer (i.e. through a union)
Closed Shop	the practice of employing only union members—made illegal under the Taft-Hartley Act
Collective Bargaining	Collective bargaining is a negotiation process between the union and employer about wages and other conditions of employment. (If a company wants to change the terms of a collective bargaining agreement while it is in effect, it must give sixty days' notice.)
Executive Order 10988	This EO, signed by President Kennedy, allows federal employees to collectively bargain with management.
Lockout	A lockout is the act of an employer closing a facility to coerce workers to meet a demand.
Open Shop	the practice of employing people without respect to union membership
Picketing	The public protest of an employer by workers (and the discouragement of non-striking workers and customers to enter the business), picketing typically takes place during a strike (when the bargaining unit refuses to work until a collective bargaining agreement is made.)
Right-to-Work Law	These laws prohibits or limits union agreements that require employees' membership, or payment of union dues or fees, as a condition of employment; they do not provide a general guarantee of employment.
Seniority	A worker's tenure; according to union contracts, seniority frequently determines whether an employee is laid off and how soon he or she may be reinstated.

Taft-Hartley Act	This Act limited the reach and influence of the NLRA; it outlawed the closed shop and certain strike and boycott activity; it allows states to pass right-to-work laws and sets up mechanisms for decertifying unions. It limited who is covered under NLRA and provided stricter rules for unions seeking the assistance of the National Labor Relations Board.
Unfair Labor Practices	According to the NLRA and Taft-Hartley, these include any discrimination, coercion, or intimidation by labor or management. Management cannot use intimidation or other forceful tactics to discourage employees from joining unions; similarly, unions cannot pressure workers to join.
Union Security Clause	part of collective bargaining agreements specifying a union shop, maintenance of membership, or an agency shop
Union Shop	a place of employment in which each member of the bargaining unit must join the union after a specified period

DISPUTE RESOLUTION

A major activity in employee relations is the management of **EMPLOYEE COMPLAINTS AND GRIEVANCES**. Complaints are generally less serious or severe than grievances, but both require timely and thoughtful action.

Complaints

Employee complaints can range from the type of coffee provided to the management style of one's boss. Some complaints are quickly and easily resolved by management or HR, while other complaints require more time, effort, and patience. Employee complaints can provide HR and management with useful information. They alert management to a problem before it grows out of control, and they give management a chance to respond and display commitment to addressing employee concerns.

When a manager or HR professional is presented with a complaint, he or she should listen carefully and openly to identify the concern behind the complaint. Asking pointed questions to gather facts will help to determine a proper plan of action. If other employees share the concern, obtaining their perspective will help to detect widespread problems. During this process, it is important to acknowledge the problem and clarify the action being taken. If action is not being taken on the complaint, it is appropriate to explain why. Demonstrating follow-through is essential to maintaining employee trust.

While complaints are inevitable, there are methods to minimize employee complaints. HR professionals can encourage managers to give ongoing feedback on performance and set clear expectations for the role. Employees can be encouraged to provide input on their work and on specific topics. (However, this should be done with care as not to encourage more complaining.) Granted, not every employee is going to be satisfied with every action taken in an organization, but it is important not to penalize legitimate complainants—such an action could silence a valuable source of information. On the other hand, if an employee makes petty complaints on a regular basis, it is essential to have a frank conversation as to how the complaining is harming the morale of the organization (if it is) and explain that the manner in which he or she is complaining is unacceptable.

Grievances

When employees believe that a company policy, collective bargaining agreement, or law has been violated, they may make a formal complaint called a grievance. **GRIEVANCES** require immediate attention. A prompt response that results in a quick resolution of the grievance will improve employee morale and productivity, and can potentially prevent costly legal action.

It is imperative to take all grievances seriously, even if they may not seem valid. HR can test the validity of a grievance by obtaining all relevant facts, as follows:

1. Actively listen to the person with the grievance. Ask follow-up questions and get concrete examples, dates, times, witnesses, and other alleged facts.

2. Consult with an employment attorney or union steward. It is important that careful steps be taken when validating a grievance. In unionized environments, the collective bargaining agreement may outline specific steps.

3. Interview potential witnesses, as appropriate, to obtain their perspective on the situation.

4. Provide an update to the person who submitted the grievance. If it seems that there is a problem that needs further investigation or action, specify what will be done. If the grievance does not seem valid, explain what was done up to this point, and why no further action will be taken.

5. If it is valid, take action to rectify the situation.

To take action on grievances:

1. If the organization has a collective bargaining agreement, follow the guidelines within it for handling grievances (and with the assistance of a union steward). Otherwise,

refer to the employee handbook if there is a specific policy or procedure outlined.

2. Complainants and their supervisors should try to resolve the problem through discussion, which may be facilitated by HR.

3. If no resolution is met, the next higher level of management may speak with the employee, without repercussions. Again, this may also be facilitated by HR.

4. During any part of this process, HR may take a more active approach as a mediator. In some cases, however, a third-party arbitrator (outside of the organization) may be used.

There are steps an organization can take to minimize its risk of employee grievances. It is important to maintain a dialogue with employees and be open to feedback. There should be a system in place where employees can file legitimate complaints before they become bigger and unmanageable. Having a clear policy on submitting grievances, and detailing how the employer will handle grievances, will promote open communication. When employees complain, it is important not to retaliate. While not every complaint may be acted upon, it is important to acknowledge the concerns and feelings of employees and to clearly communicate what action will or will not be taken and why.

EMPLOYEE DISCIPLINE AND TERMINATIONS

Most employees strive to do well at their jobs, but sometimes they do not meet the expectations of the job or exhibit behaviors that are unacceptable. When this happens, most managers use an approach called progressive discipline, a series of steps that offers the employee opportunities to improve. If the employee does not improve during one step, then he or she progresses to the next step, which is considered more severe and moves closer to termination.

The Steps of Progressive Discipline

The number and details of each step in PROGRESSIVE DISCIPLINE vary from employer to employer. Some employers, especially those subject to collective bargaining agreements, require a strict use of each step in succession. Others, however, reserve the right to use any or all steps necessary to address a particular issue. For example, not following the company's dress code may subject an employee to a verbal warning, but physical violence toward another employee will likely result in immediate termination. Taking steps of progressive discipline is typically useful for repetitive, non-serious offenses or when there is no indication of improvement by the employee. Below are typical steps found in a progressive discipline procedure.

A **VERBAL WARNING** is the least serious consequence of a poor behavior. It involves a conversation between a supervisor an employee, in which the inappropriate behavior is identified and expectations for improvement are made clear.

A **WRITTEN WARNING** is appropriate when the employee ignores a verbal warning about his or her behavior or does not show improvement. The written warning, or "write-up," documents the incident, explains why the behavior is inappropriate (and references applicable company policies), explains what changes are expected, and describes the consequences of the continued behavior. Typically, an employee is asked to sign a copy to acknowledge receipt, although a signature may not necessarily mean the employee agrees with the contents of the write-up.

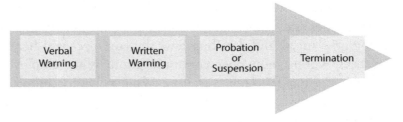

Figure 5.1. Typical Progressive Discipline Procedure

A **PERFORMANCE IMPROVEMENT PLAN** places the employee on **PROBATION** and requires specific actions to be taken in order to meet the supervisor's expectations. The employee is required to follow the plan and to show improvement as a condition of continued employment.

Suspension

A **SUSPENSION**, if used, is often the final step before termination. A suspension lasts a certain duration, may be paid or unpaid, and is accompanied by a document that outlines the terms of the suspension, specific steps that need to be taken to correct the issue, and the consequences for not improving. When the employee completes the suspension, he or she typically receives one last chance to demonstrate improvement.

Termination

TERMINATION OF EMPLOYMENT (or firing) is the final step in the progressive discipline process when behavioral problems are continual, or the employee commits gross misconduct such as theft or violence. Usually a firing is immediate, but should not be a surprise if the employer has clearly conveyed expectations and provided ongoing feedback to the employee.

There are other steps for progressive discipline that may be used, including demotions, temporary pay cuts, reassignments, and required training. Whatever methods are used, they should fit the behavior and resolve the problem rather than simply provide a route toward termination. Being open and frank during each step of the process can help the employee improve.

SAFETY AND HEALTH

Organizations have a responsibility to protect the safety, health, and well-being of their employees. Ensuring safety and health is a moral obligation due to its humanitarian nature. At the same time, an employer has legal obligations to ensure employee safety and health; employers must follow specific guidelines under these laws and face certain penalties and fines if they do not. Taking the necessary precautions can also reduce costs the business may incur, including the costs of medical care, sick leave, disability benefits, and lost productivity.

Depending on the nature of the business and where it conducts its operations, there are a number of health and safety hazards and risks that employees may face. A workplace **HAZARD** is something that can cause harm if it is not mitigated or eliminated. **RISK** is defined as the probability that a specific outcome (or in this context, harm) will occur. It is the role of HR professionals or safety professionals to identify hazards and assess risks that affect employees for the moral, legal, and financial reasons described above.

In general, there are three categories of workplace hazards that are described below: physical, chemical, and psychosocial. Some industries may be more prone to certain hazards than others. For example, the construction industry may have more physical than chemical hazards, while the financial industry may have numerous psychosocial hazards but very few physical hazards.

Table 5.2. Workplace Hazards

physical hazards	heavy machinery
	slippery surfaces
	hot temperature or surfaces
	confined spaces
	extreme heights
chemical hazards	viruses
	bacteria
	mold
	blood-borne pathogens
	acids
	vapors
	fire
	explosions

psychosocial hazards	job insecurity
	poor work-life balance
	high demands
	long work hours
	unfair working conditions

HR and safety officers can take measures to mitigate workplace hazards. They should develop methods and procedures to manage hazards that can cause injury to their workers and their facilities. Workspaces, equipment, procedures, and services should periodically be evaluated for safety, and employees should be actively included in developing safe working practices. Resources should be allocated to train employees on safety and to enforce safety rules. Safety rules and procedures should be regularly evaluated for their effectiveness, with management and employee input.

Effective safety officers must be well versed in those laws and regulations that govern employee health and safety (such as the Organizational Safety and Health Act) as well as industry standards on best practices. They need to be able to design operational procedures as well as recordkeeping systems for clarity and accountability. They should also be able to identify and implement the safety equipment and resources necessary to protect employees as they conduct their jobs.

Security

Just as a home needs to be secure from intruders, an organization also has SECURITY needs. A data breach, for example, can lead to key information being leaked to competitors and harm the organization financially. An intruder breaking in to the company's headquarters can steal important records, potentially resulting in financial or other losses. Protecting the physical security of the organization's employees, facilities, infrastructure, and resources is vital to its survival. An organization should carefully plan its security strategy.

Figure 5.2. Components of Organizational Security

1. Develop security policies and procedures that are well documented and accessible to all employees. This documentation shows the organization's commitment to security and clarifies procedures to management, which enforces security concerns on a day-to-day basis.

2. Maintain a physically secure environment. If the business is at risk of theft, robberies, violence, or other crimes, it is important to install surveillance, secure entries, metal detectors, and other devices to monitor the premises and prevent security breaches. The organization should also have policies and procedures regarding employees' handling of company equipment, including computers. The policies should clearly indicate what steps the employee should take when company property is lost or stolen, so that the organization can respond appropriately and mitigate the effects of that loss.

3. Restrict information only to those who need to know it. Employees should only have access to the files, records, and information necessary to conduct their jobs. In particular, limit access to sensitive information only to those who need it in order to perform a certain function or who are in a position to make decisions related to that information. Additionally, the company should have a policy requiring employees to protect the confidentiality of any sensitive or proprietary information to which they have access.

4. Protect data from loss, theft, or intrusion. Viruses, malware, and cyber-attacks threaten an organization's technological infrastructure. The organization should install the appropriate firewalls, anti-virus software, and network monitoring software necessary to protect its infrastructure from attacks. Employees should be required to maintain strong computer and network passwords; these passwords should be changed regularly. The organization should have "acceptable use" policies restricting employees from accessing non-work related websites (to minimize inadvertent downloads that can be harmful to their computer or even the entire network); this can usually be achieved by installing web filtering software on the network.

5. Protect financial assets from loss or theft. If the company interacts with the general public and employees have access to certain cash reserves, protocols should be in place to monitor the flow of money and require employees to balance cash at the end of their shifts. The company should also protect any reserves it has on-site by using a safe, and it should limit the funds it keeps on the

premises to only the amount necessary to conduct daily business.

6. Train employees on security practices and hold them accountable. Poor training often leads to security breaches, and thorough training conducted periodically will keep employees aware and invested in the security of the business.

PRIVACY AND CONFIDENTIALITY

Managing an organization's safety and security can prompt **PRIVACY** concerns. The organization needs to carefully monitor and protect its assets; however, employees desire a degree of privacy in their daily activities. To manage risk, organizations may take measures like monitoring computer usage, conducting background checks of employees, and tracking people who enter and exit facilities. In general, employees in the US should have no broad expectation of privacy, and the employer has a right to monitor and protect its assets. However, there are federal and state laws that protect the privacy of employees to some extent. When implementing certain measures, it is important for the organization to understand whether the activity is lawful and to weigh how effectively each practice achieves a specific business need.

Protected Information

As a rule, only personally identifiable information such as a person's name or Social Security number is afforded special protection by data privacy laws. In some cases, a combination of information such as birth date, address, and gender can be used to identify an individual and is therefore considered protected information. There are federal and state laws that govern the usage and sharing of personally identifiable information:

- The **HEALTH INSURANCE PORTABILITY AND ACCOUNTABILITY ACT (HIPAA)** protects health-related information with covered entities such as insurance plans.

- The **GENETIC INFORMATION NON-DISCRIMINATION ACT (GINA)** protects and restricts the usage of employees' genetic information.

The Fair Credit Reporting Act requires employers to obtain written permission from applicants before conducting credit checks.

- The **FAIR CREDIT REPORTING ACT (FCRA)** restricts the ways that consumer data, such as credit reports, may be used for employment purposes.

Many US states have their own laws concerning data security and notifications of breaches, and organizations should be aware of all data security laws in the states in which they operate. Additionally, companies have a responsibility under the law to protect not only employee information, but also that of job applicants, independent contractors, and customers. Companies that operate internationally should also be aware of the laws of each country in which they operate and implement the most stringent security mechanisms to comply with all laws necessary. Even if there is no law that specifically requires the protection of certain data, it is still a best practice for the organization to ensure that all personal information, whether protected or not protected by law, is safe. Keeping active employees' data secure and discarding data that is no longer needed (as allowed by recordkeeping laws and regulations) can help mitigate the organization's risk. Employers can also protect data by disclosing it only to parties on a need-to-know basis, with the explicit authorization of the employee, or by virtue of a court order. Data should be provided using the most secure means possible, such as encrypted email, and there should be specific procedures in place if a data breach occurs. Because HR professionals often work with personal data on a regular basis, it is important that they maintain CONFIDENTIALITY to the greatest extent possible and take careful measures not to compromise the security of data.

Workplace Monitoring and Searches

It is common for employers to MONITOR the computer, email, web, and phone usage of employees for quality control and security. They may also implement drug and alcohol testing to ensure the safety of employees and to prevent accidents or injuries.

As a best practice, and to comply with various privacy laws, the organization should notify employees (typically in a handbook) that they should have no expectation of privacy when on the premises or when using company resources and of the specific ways in which the company may monitor employees. Companies should contact a qualified attorney to understand the legal limits of employee surveillance, drug testing, and personal searches. For example, companies may not put cameras in restrooms, but they may use cameras to monitor a cash register. Employers may also be limited in conduct of personal SEARCHES and may not force employees to submit to a search; however, they may rightfully terminate employees who refuse.

Clear policies that are applied consistently to all employees will help the organization set expectations and manage risk. If employees understand what is expected of them as well as the consequences for non-compliance, and if they understand that the rules are enforced universally, the organization can protect itself against claims of unfair treatment or discrimination while promoting a safe workplace.

GLOBAL EMPLOYEE RELATIONS

Many organizations operate in a global environment where employment issues, employment laws, and business practices can vary dramatically from country to country. HR professionals working in multinational companies must have a global perspective a solid grasp of international employment issues to help the organization run smoothly. For multinational employers, there are unique employee relations issues to manage. Employees abroad may have unique health and safety issues due to political or economic conditions, regulations, or the physical environment. Additionally, the employer must also comply with the laws of the countries in which it operates.

Global Health and Safety

Addressing safety and health issues is an important HR function. Employees working abroad may not enjoy the same quality of healthcare or environmental safety as those working in the United States. HR practitioners develop policies and employment benefits to support these employees. For example, companies may offer private insurance plans or funds for medical assistance to protect the health of employees. However, policies must comply with the country's laws and should be a generally accepted business practice in that country.

Depending on the regions in which they operate, international organizations may also have to address kidnapping, harassment, extortion, and other violence in regions experiencing political unrest. These dangers can occur either on or near the worksite or in residential areas. To protect employees working in dangerous areas, many firms provide bodyguards, change travel routes to make it difficult for criminals to track an individual, and provide safety training for family members of employees. Some companies may secure the grounds of their facilities with fences, barricades, armed guards, metal detectors, and/or surveillance devices. Others may take steps to minimize the visibility of the company.

To ensure the safety of expatriates (i.e. foreign nationals working abroad), the company may provide emergency protective services through an organization that can refer the ill or injured employee to adequate medical care if available locally, dispatch physicians, or transport employees to safety via aircraft. Additional safeguards may include in-country legal counsel or emergency cash for medical expenses or travel home.

Cultural Differences in the Workplace

Cultural norms in a country or region influence how people act and interact with one another. When employing international workers, the organization should be clear about its expectations of all its workers, regardless of geography. At the same time, in order to sustain successful operations in a country, an employer should understand the norms, values, and attitudes of the workers there. If the organization's values are completely contrary to the culture of a region or country, conflict may arise if the situation is not properly managed. Providing flexibility for certain cultural practices while taking meaningful action to assimilate employees into the organization can alleviate tensions. Cultural differences among international employees may include different attitudes toward work. HR practitioners and management must recognize these differences and understand how they affect intra-company relations. HR practitioners can play a key role in facilitating open dialogue and providing learning opportunities for both US and non-US employees to work together more effectively.

Global Labor Relations

The impact and nature of labor unions varies from country to country. In some places unions do not exist or are relatively weak. Elsewhere unions are extremely strong and may be closely aligned with political parties—Europe is one example. In other places, such as the United States, unions have declined in influence and membership over time. These differences affect how collective bargaining occurs, too. In the United States, independent unions bargain with the employer over working conditions and wages. In Europe, however, bargaining is typically done industry-wide or regionally. Some countries require that companies have union representatives on their boards of directors (co-determination)[1]. It is important for multinational organizations to understand the norms of a country and be prepared to work with organized labor where it is present, in the manner that is customary for that country or region.

REVIEW

Main Ideas to Remember

- The term *employee relations* refers to the maintenance of employer-employee relationships to ensure high productivity and morale. Effective employee relations improve employees' understanding of the organization's policies, procedures, and expectations. Employee relations address conflict, poor behavior, and difficult situations; this field also identifies ways to both prevent and resolve these problems.

- The employee's manager or department may have his or her own specific procedures and expectations that are typically aligned with those of the overall organization. When employees perform poorly or behave in an unacceptable manner, the manager will identify the issues, counsel the employee, and discuss a plan to correct the problem.

- When an employee files a complaint about his or her work conditions, management or HR will discuss the concerns, investigate if necessary, and collect key data to make an informed decision. In serious situations such as sexual harassment or discrimination, employees are typically reminded of their grievance and appeal rights and discrimination, as well as any whistleblower protections.

- Organizational culture is the workplace environment fostered by both leadership and employees. It describes how people within the organization interact with one another, and it is affected by the experiences, personalities, values, beliefs, and principles of leadership and employees. An organization's culture affects its overall identity—the way that employees, clients, and the general public perceive it.

- There are over 180 federal laws that apply to numerous employment contexts, including specific industries and sizes of companies; the US Department of Labor (DOL) administers and enforces these laws and the mandates and regulations that implement them.

- According to the Fair Labor Standards Act (FLSA), most private and public employers must pay a minimum federal wage and overtime pay of one and one-half times the regular rate of pay, or time and a half.

- The Occupational Safety and Health Act regulates the safety and health of employees; it is administered by the Occupational Safety and Health Administration (OSHA), which may conduct inspections and investigations of those employers covered by the Act, who are responsible for ensuring a safe work environment for employees, in compliance with health and safety standards.

- The Uniformed Services Employment and Reemployment Rights Act (USERRA) allows certain employees the right to reemployment following an absence from work due to military service, including those serving in the reserves and the National Guard.

- The Employee Polygraph Protection Act allows polygraph tests in only a few circumstances; otherwise, employers are not permitted to use polygraphs on employees.

- Many labor-related, public safety and environmental laws, usually enforced by OSHA, protect WHISTLEBLOWERS—employees who report violations of labor laws. OSHA may ensure that whistleblowers who face employer retaliation receive payment of back wages or job reinstatement.

- Specific labor laws apply to government contractors or employers receiving government grants, including the Davis-Bacon Act, the McNamara-O'Hara Service Contract Act, and the Walsh-Healy Public Contracts Act. Government contractors must comply with federal affirmative action and equal opportunity laws, executive orders, and regulations.

- Individual states (and sometimes localities) create and enforce their own laws related to the employment of workers. Employers should be aware of the employment laws in all states in which they conduct business and employment; the state's Department of Labor can be contacted for state-specific information about employment laws.

- An employee handbook, also referred to as an employee manual, is a document of the organization's policies and procedures that affect all employees. It can provide both employment and practical information like company rules, performance expectations, and office operations. A written employee handbook provides employees with clear guidance, explains organizational expectations, and fosters a culture in which problems are addressed fairly and consistently.

- An employment-at-will statement specifies that an employee or employer may terminate the employment relationship, with or without reason, and with or without notice. In an at-will employment situation (which is the case in many states), there is no expectation of employment either indefinitely or for a specified duration.

- Handbooks can be a useful tool in situations when corrective action needs to be taken with an employee, including termination of employment. When disciplining or terminating employees, it is helpful to refer to the specific policy or policies being violated.

- The term labor relations describes the interaction between employers and employees, typically in a unionized environment. (However, in some cases it applies to non-union workers as well.) When labor relations are strong at an organization, management works effectively with employee representatives (typically labor unions) to solve problems in the interests of both the employees and the organization.

- The National Labor Relations Act of 1935 (also called the Wagner Act) granted most private-sector workers many labor rights, including the right to strike, to bargain as a union, and to protest the conditions of their employment.

- Employees covered by the Wagner Act are granted certain rights to join together to improve their wages and working conditions, with or without a union. This means that although a union may not be present in an organization, employees at that organization still have the right to discuss the conditions of their employment and take action as a group.

- Concerted activity occurs when two or more employees take action for their mutual benefit or protection with respect to the conditions or terms of their employment. It is protected by the NLRA.

- The effects of the NLRA were changed substantially when the Taft-Hartley Act was passed in 1947. Taft-Hartley outlawed closed shops, jurisdictional strikes, and secondary boycotts. It set up mechanisms for decertifying unions and allowed states to pass certain anti-union legislation such as right-to-work laws. The effects of the NLRA were changed substantially when the Taft-Hartley Act was passed in 1947.

- Employee complaints can range in scope, but generally are not severe. They can alert management to a problem before it grows out of control, and they give management a chance to respond and display commitment to addressing employee concerns.

- Grievances are formal complaints warning HR and management about major problems requiring immediate attention. A prompt response that results in a quick resolution will improve employee morale and productivity and can potentially prevent costly legal action.

- Progressive discipline is typically useful for repetitive, non-serious offenses when there is no indication of improvement by the employee. These steps include verbal warning, written warning, probation, suspension, and termination. Some employers, especially those subject to collective bargaining agreements, require a strict use of each step in succession. Others reserve the right to use any or all steps necessary to address a particular issue.

- Multinational employers address unique employee relations issues. Employees abroad face particular health and safety issues due to political or economic conditions, regulations, or the physical environment; HR must address these. The employer must also comply with the laws of the countries in which it operates.

- Organizations have a responsibility to protect the safety, health, and well-being of their employees. Ensuring safety and health is a moral obligation due to its humanitarian nature. At the same time, an employer has legal obligations to ensure employee safety and health; employers must follow specific guidelines under these laws and face certain penalties and fines if they do not.

- A workplace hazard is something that can cause harm if it is not mitigated or eliminated. It is the role of HR professionals or safety professionals to identify hazards and assess risks that affect employees.

- There are three categories of workplace hazards: physical, chemical, and psychosocial. Some industries may be more prone to certain hazards than others.

- HR and safety officers can take a series of measures to mitigate workplace hazards. They should develop methods and procedures to manage hazards that can cause injury to their workers and their facilities. Workspaces, equipment, procedures, and services should periodically be evaluated for safety, and employees should be actively included in developing safe working practices. Resources should be allocated to train employees on safety and to enforce safety rules. Safety rules and procedures should be regularly evaluated for their effectiveness, with management and employee input.

- To manage risk, organizations may take measures like monitoring computer usage, conducting background checks of employees, and tracking people who enter and exit facilities. These activities, however, can lead to privacy concerns. Companies should weigh the effectiveness of these measures and understand their legality.

Key Terms to Review

- agency shop
- arbitration
- bargaining unit
- closed shop
- COBRA
- collective bargaining
- complaint
- concerted activity
- confidentiality
- Consumer Credit Protection Act
- Davis-Bacon Act
- employee handbook
- Employee Polygraph Protection Act
- employee relations
- employment-at-will
- ERISA
- Executive Order 10988
- Fair Credit Reporting Act (FCRA)
- Fair Labor Standards Act (FLSA)
- Family and Medical Leave Act (FMLA)
- Genetic Information Non-discrimination Act (GINA)
- grievance
- hazard
- HIPAA
- labor relations
- labor union
- lockout
- McNamara-O'Hara Service Contract Act
- National Labor Relations Act of 1935
- Occupational Safety and Health Act
- Office of Federal Contract Compliance Programs (OFCCP)
- open shop
- organizational culture
- Patient Protection and Affordable Care Act
- performance improvement plan
- picketing
- privacy
- probation
- progressive discipline
- right-to-work laws
- risk
- seniority
- suspension
- Taft-Hartley Act
- termination of employment
- types of hazards
- unfair labor practice
- union security clause
- union shop
- USERRA
- verbal warning
- Wagner Act
- Walsh-Healy Public Contracts Act
- Worker Adjustment and Retraining Notification Act (WARN)
- workplace monitoring
- workplace searches
- whistleblower
- written warning

6

PRACTICE TEST

1. Leadership theories that look at the personal characteristics of a leader are:

A) trait theories

B) situational theories

C) behavioral theories

D) contingency theories

2. To be effective, company goals must—

A) require the participation of line staff

B) be available in multiple languages

C) grow the company

D) be specific and measurable

3. The party responsible for verifying that an employee is eligible to work in the United States is:

A) USCIS

B) the Department of Labor

C) the employer

D) the employee

4. What is employee training?

A) the development of skills that apply to an employee's job

B) teaching employees about their requirements

C) one-on-one tutoring

D) an intervention of employees who need special attention

5. An employer has the right to—

A) forbid employees from discussing union membership or activities

B) terminate two non-union employees for discussing the conditions of their job

C) describe a union's strike history and the economic consequences of strikes

D) give preferential treatment to one union over another

6. Which of the following HR responsibilities is most likely to differ from country to country?

A) job analysis

B) training and development

C) compensation and benefits

D) personnel records

7. The *prudent person rule* is associated with which law?

A) FLSA

B) ERISA

C) FMLA

D) OSHA

8. Which of the following strategies is associated with workforce expansion?

   A) outsourcing

   B) demotions

   C) management training

   D) job rotations

9. Which is generally true about executive compensation?

   A) Executives receive a wider variety of compensation than other employees.

   B) Executives receive cheaper health insurance than other employees.

   C) Executives are guaranteed pay even if they do not work.

   D) Executives do not receive a base salary.

10. The Civil Rights Act of 1964 does not prohibit discrimination on which of the following?

    A) color

    B) religion

    C) race

    D) age

11. Which of the following career development strategies best promotes a wide range of skills?

    A) job rotation

    B) job shadowing

    C) job sharing

    D) flexible work arrangements

12. Workers' Compensation provides benefits for:

    A) dependents in the event of the employee's death

    B) pregnancy

    C) job-related injuries or death

    D) retirement

13. Which of the following benefits is not required by law?

    A) life insurance

    B) health insurance

    C) retirement plan

    D) all of the above

14. A written description of the work performed by an employee is called a/an:

    A) job specification

    B) job description

    C) at-will employment statement

    D) compensation analysis

15. The primary purpose of an HR audit is to—

    A) provide information to the federal government

    B) determine how many HR staff are needed

    C) evaluate the effectiveness of the HR function

    D) determine which HRIS system to use

16. Which of the following statements about affirmative action plans is true?

    A) All employers with over 100 employees are required to have an AAP.

    B) An AAP is required for employers who have been found to discriminate against employees.

    C) An AAP is required by the Fair Labor Standards Act.

    D) An AAP must be signed by a company officer and made available to internal employees and vendors.

17. The least serious OSHA violation is:

    A) serious

    B) other-than-serious

    C) de minimus

    D) non-qualified

18. Which federal agency has the primary responsibility to enforce employment non-discrimination laws?

    A) Department of Labor

    B) Equal Employment Opportunity Commission

    C) National Association for the Advancement of Colored People

    D) Office of the Attorney General

19. COBRA allows a terminated employee to continue coverage under the employer's health insurance policy for how long?

    A) 12 months

    B) 18 months

    C) 36 months

    D) indefinitely

20. Which types of employees cannot be represented by a union under the NLRA?

    A) supervisors, confidential employees, and managers

    B) seasonal employees, managers, and supervisors

    C) supervisors and key employees

    D) managers, supervisors, and non-US citizens

21. The two primary dimensions of behavioral theories of leadership are:

    A) common sense and task-relevant knowledge

    B) consideration and initiating structure

    C) self-confidence and initiating structure

    D) initiating structure and task-relevant knowledge

22. Which of the following laws allows employers to establish drug testing policies?

    A) Occupational Safety and Health Act

    B) Drug Free Workplace Act

    C) Equal Employment Opportunity

    D) Drug Testing Act

23. A consistent wage despite the number of hours worked is called:

    A) salary

    B) bonus

    C) variable pay

    D) base pay

24. Which of the following factors is considered in an environmental scan?

    A) competition

    B) succession plan

    C) staffing metrics

    D) compensation analysis

25. Which of the following laws deals directly with pay discrimination?

    A) Fair Labor Standards Act

    B) Affirmative Action

    C) PPACA

    D) Equal Pay Act

26. The centralized approach to compensation works best when—

    A) the company wants to pay the same wages to US and non-US employees

    B) the other countries have a low standard of living

    C) there are few international employees

    D) inflation is low

27. Which of the following is typically considered a taxable benefit?

    A) vacation pay

    B) health insurance

    C) flexible spending account

    D) 401(k) matching contribution

28. Which of the following recruitment methods is likely to result in greater loyalty?

    A) campus recruiting

    B) internet job board

    C) employee referrals

    D) newspaper ad

29. The Fair Credit Reporting Act requires an employer to—

A) obtain written authorization from an applicant before conducting a credit check

B) use credit checks to verify an applicant's eligibility to work

C) conduct a credit check secretly

D) provide verbal notification that a credit check will be completed on a prospective employee

30. Disparate treatment occurs when—

A) a neutral compensation practice results in unintentional wage discrimination

B) affirmative action plans are put into place

C) an employee who is a member of a protected class is intentionally paid less

D) employees are all eligible for pay-for-performance compensation

31. What is the main purpose of a grievance procedure?

A) to resolve conflict

B) to empower employees to go on strike

C) to terminate employees

D) to provide progressive discipline

32. *Reasonable accommodation* is a term associated with which federal statute?

A) Americans with Disabilities Act

B) Civil Rights Act of 1964

C) Wagner Act

D) Fair Labor Standards Act

33. Which type of learning curve gradually increases in pace with larger increments?

A) S-shaped learning curve

B) positively accelerating learning curve

C) negatively accelerating learning curve

D) plateau

34. What is the last and final step of a grievance procedure?

A) NLRB ruling

B) third-party arbitration

C) union representative and management

D) strike

35. What is the core of labor relations?

A) collective bargaining

B) union dues

C) right-to-work laws

D) strikes and lock-outs

36. The Family and Medical Leave Act requires employers to—

A) provide affordable health insurance to employees and their dependents

B) provide employees with up to twelve weeks of paid leave for surgeries and sickness

C) provide Workers' Compensation insurance to employees who are injured on the job

D) give employees up to twelve weeks of unpaid leave to care for themselves or a family member with a serious health condition

37. Employment at will means that—

A) the employee is guaranteed a job only for a specified amount of time

B) the employee or employer may terminate the relationship at any time

C) employees may only be fired for serious offenses

D) employees must have an employment contract with the employer

38. Which agency is responsible for enforcing federal laws regarding safety on the job?

A) Bureau of Labor Statistics

B) Department of Commerce

C) Occupational Safety and Health Administration

D) USCIS

39. Which is not a category of exempt status under the Fair Labor Standards Act?

  A) outside sales

  B) management

  C) hourly assistants

  D) executives

40. Which is not one of the criteria for evaluating training programs?

  A) synthesis

  B) reactions

  C) learning

  D) behavior

41. Which of the following federal laws applies to most employers?

  A) Rehabilitation Act of 1973

  B) Vietnam-Era Veterans Readjustment Act

  C) Age Discrimination in Employment Act

  D) Affirmative Action

42. A company wants to restructure a department. Which task would HR likely not conduct?

  A) developing a project plan for handling the restructuring

  B) designing new products and services

  C) writing job descriptions for the new or refined positions

  D) assessing the skills and competencies of staff

43. An organization has many detailed procedures and is resistant to change. Which phase of the organizational life cycle does this describe?

  A) birth

  B) growth

  C) maturity

  D) decline

44. How long must employers keep records of occupational illnesses, injuries, and incidents?

  A) one year

  B) five years

  C) ten years

  D) indefinitely

45. What is the purpose of an employee assistance program?

  A) to provide free, confidential counseling on work-life and personal matters

  B) to assist employees with finding a job when they are laid off

  C) to help employers find the best candidates for a position

  D) to provide legal counsel to employees who want to sue the company

46. The primary reason employee handbooks should be reviewed carefully and continually updated is because they may—

  A) be available to the public for review

  B) create an enforceable contract

  C) provide new employees with important information

  D) be the only way the employer communicates with employees

47. Decentralization works best in organizations where—

  A) employees dislike management

  B) unions are present

  C) the organization is too top-heavy

  D) a quick response to problems is needed

48. An employee removes his safety glasses because they are uncomfortable. He gets a chemical in his eye and requires medical treatment. This is an example of which of the following?

  A) unsafe act

  B) unfair treatment

  C) organizational risk

  D) unsafe work environment

49. ERISA was designed to protect employee rights in what area?

A) retirement plans

B) unemployment compensation

C) workers' compensation

D) recruitment and hiring

50. Which are terms associated with selecting a market position for base salaries?

A) lead

B) match

C) lag

D) all the above

51. A practitioner with expertise in a limited area of human resources is called:

A) HR generalist

B) HR manager

C) HR specialist

D) none of the above

52. Who does not typically appraise an employee's performance in a 360-degree performance appraisal system?

A) peers

B) subordinates

C) current supervisor

D) none of the above

53. Behavioral-based training includes all of the following except:

A) diversity training

B) internship

C) case studies/incidents

D) business games

54. What is the main reason employers offer a comprehensive benefits package?

A) to reduce operating costs

B) to do what other companies are doing

C) to help attract and retain employees

D) to save money on taxes

55. Which form of compensation is typically reserved for executives?

A) base pay

B) bonus

C) stock options

D) differential pay

56. The FMLA requires employers having ___ employees within a fifty-mile radius to provide job-protected leave to qualified employees for medical reasons.

A) 10

B) 25

C) 50

D) 100

57. Which law governs the number of hours that children may work?

A) FLSA

B) ADEA

C) FMLA

D) IRCA

58. If a non-exempt employee is off for Memorial Day but works ten hours a day the rest of the week, how many hours of overtime pay is she entitled to under the FLSA?

A) 0

B) 8

C) 40

D) 48

59. Which of the following is not a type of retirement plan?

A) defined contribution plan

B) defined benefit plan

C) defined retirement age plan

D) profit sharing plan

60. Which is an example(s) of pay for performance?

   A) variable pay

   B) piecework

   C) gainsharing

   D) all of the above

61. Health insurance benefits are a component of:

   A) total rewards

   B) organizational development

   C) work-life balance

   D) pay for performance

62. Title VII allows an employer to discriminate on the basis of sex, religion, or national origin if these are a *bona fide occupational qualification*. Which job might apply?

   A) teacher

   B) doctor

   C) fashion model

   D) police officer

63. The OSHA Form 300 must be completed—

   A) when an employee dies due to a work-related illness or injury

   B) when a work-related injury leads to missed days

   C) when a work-related injury requires medical care beyond first aid

   D) all of the above

64. How much notice must a company give the bargaining unit if it wants to change the terms of a collective bargaining agreement while it is in effect?

   A) 30 days

   B) 60 days

   C) 90 days

   D) 120 days

65. Which of the following activities is typical of the transactional leader?

   A) allows workers to be autonomous

   B) gets involved when standards are not met

   C) micromanages employees

   D) sets unrealistic expectations

66. An applicant applying for which of the following positions may be required to take a polygraph test?

   A) a teacher working with small children

   B) a cashier at a grocery store

   C) an agent at an insurance company

   D) a delivery driver for a pharmaceutical company

67. A closed shop is a company that does which of the following?

   A) refuses to hire union members

   B) requires employees to become union members

   C) sponsors a union

   D) applies to all unionized workplaces

68. What theory includes the elements of safety and security needs and self-actualization?

   A) Maslow's hierarchy of needs

   B) Myers Briggs

   C) Leadership theory

   D) Equality theory

69. Which is a method of comparing the relative performance of employees?

   A) structuring

   B) pay for performance

   C) ranking

   D) performance improvement plan

70. Which document confirms an employee's identity and verifies his/her right to work in the United States, for purposes of the I-9 form?

A) unexpired US passport

B) driver's license

C) birth certificate

D) foreign passport

71. The four distinct stages for HR planning do not include:

A) action plans

B) HR systems analysis

C) environmental scanning

D) forecasting

72. What is the difference between Affirmative Action and Equal Employment Opportunity?

A) Equal Employment Opportunity is required by law.

B) Affirmative Action promotes fair employment classes.

C) Affirmative Action is required of government contractors.

D) Equal Employment Opportunity sets quotas for hiring.

73. Which is not part of job analysis?

A) selecting jobs to analyze

B) collecting data from incumbents

C) writing job descriptions

D) designing jobs

74. Which of the following elements is part of a company's compensation philosophy?

A) fixed and variable pay

B) pay in relation to the market

C) pay for the job

D) all of the above

75. Strategic HR management includes the following activity:

A) planning

B) developing objectives

C) aligning resources

D) all of the above

76. Which would be considered a bona fide occupational requirement for firefighters?

A) applicants must be at least 5'5"

B) applicants must be able to handle extreme temperatures

C) applicants must be US citizens

D) applicants must have an bachelor's degree

77. What is the main purpose of the Davis-Bacon Act of 1931?

A) It requires federal contractors to implement affirmative action plans.

B) It prohibits discrimination on the basis of age of those over fifty years old.

C) It requires certain federal contractors to pay a prevailing wage to employees.

D) It requires the payment of overtime to non-exempt employees.

78. Which law protects employees covered by private pension programs?

A) Employee Retirement Income Security Act

B) Fair Credit Reporting Act

C) Tax Reform Act of 1986

D) Retirement Act

79. The National Labor Relations Act was enacted in:

A) 1910

B) 1935

C) 1950

D) 1999

80. An organization's mission statement includes which of the following?

A) a statement of purpose

B) a strategic plan

C) a staffing model

D) all of the above

81. Which union security clause requires workers to join a union?

A) closed shop

B) union shop

C) open shop

D) agency shop

82. How long does an employee have to file a complaint of discrimination with the EEOC?

A) 30 days

B) 90 days

C) 180 days

D) 365 days

83. According to the FLSA, which would be calculated toward overtime pay?

A) A traffic jam causes the employee to get home an hour late.

B) The employee takes three days of paid vacation.

C) The employee travels from home to a work site in response to an emergency.

D) The employee is on call but is able to conduct personal business.

84. Which is not a requirement of the Americans with Disabilities Act (ADA)?

A) Newly built public facilities must be accessible to people with disabilities.

B) Buildings financed with public funds must be accessible to people with disabilities.

C) Employers may ask applicants to disclose their disabilities to determine if an accommodation will need to be made.

D) Employers with more than fifteen employees are required to provide reasonable accommodations to employees with disabilities.

85. Which is not an important feature of new hire onboarding?

A) determining job satisfaction

B) training staff on company policies and procedures

C) providing a tour of the facilities

D) integrating new employees into the organizational culture

86. Which learning domains influence behavior?

A) skills

B) attitude

C) knowledge

D) all of the above

87. What is a legal theory that makes employers liable for a harmful act if the employer knew about the employee's potential to cause harm?

A) reckless hiring

B) negligent hiring

C) liable hiring

D) risky hiring

88. What is the planned elimination of personnel to streamline operations?

A) acquisition

B) consolidation

C) termination

D) downsizing

89. What occurs when a neutral employment policy has a disproportionately negative effect on minorities?

A) adverse impact

B) disparate impact

C) discriminatory practice

D) personal bias

90. An election has just been held in a bargaining unit. Of the employees who voted, eighty-five percent voted for the union. However, only fifty-five percent of those who voted are actually dues-paying members of the union. Which employees do the union represent?

   A) only the dues-paying members

   B) all who voted for the union

   C) all who voted for or against the union

   D) all employees in the bargaining unit

91. Which law governs collective bargaining for federal employees?

   A) National Labor Relations Act

   B) Wagner Act

   C) Civil Service Reform Act

   D) Taft-Hartley Act

92. Americans working for an American company in Germany are referred to as—

   A) expatriates

   B) host country nationals

   C) external immigrants

   D) undocumented workers

93. Which are important activities in strategic planning?

   A) external scan

   B) internal scan

   C) SWOT analysis

   D) all of the above

94. What is an interview process called in which identical questions are asked of each candidate?

   A) structured

   B) unstructured

   C) EEO requirement

   D) open-ended

95. What type of compensation is an annual bonus?

   A) time-based

   B) direct

   C) indirect

   D) equitable

96. Progressive discipline is

   A) a "zero tolerance" policy.

   B) a system of discrimination in disciplining employees.

   C) a series of disciplinary actions that results in more severe punishment.

   D) required under the FLSA.

97. According to Herzberg's theory, which of the following is a motivation factor?

   A) personal growth

   B) relationships with coworkers

   C) job security

   D) work environment

98. Which of the following are funding models of insurance?

   A) self-funded

   B) fully insured

   C) both A and B

   D) none of the above

99. If an employee files a grievance, who typically handles it first?

   A) supervisor

   B) president/CEO

   C) arbitrator

   D) union steward

100. What is not an example of a wellness program?

   A) a smoking cessation program

   B) profit sharing

   C) a weight loss program

   D) an employee assistance program

101. Which restructuring practice broadens job scope by expanding the tasks it performs?

   A) job rotation

   B) job elimination

   C) delegation

   D) job enlargements

102. What is a payment given to employees who are laid off through no fault of their own?

   A) life insurance

   B) unemployment compensation

   C) temporary pay

   D) variable pay

103. What is an appropriate response by employers to sexual harassment complaints?

   A) a policy against sexual harassment

   B) regular training of employees on sexual harassment

   C) investigation of complaints

   D) all of the above

104. Which law prohibits mandatory retirement based on an employee's age?

   A) Americans with Disabilities Act

   B) Genetic Information Non-discrimination Act

   C) Age Discrimination in Employment Act

   D) Fair Labor Standards Act

105. What is a performance evaluation also called?

   A) a performance appraisal

   B) a write-up

   C) progressive discipline

   D) informal feedback

106. Someone who is paid below the established pay range of a job is considered:

   A) green-circled

   B) red-circled

   C) purple-circled

   D) non-circled

107. Salary compression occurs when—

   A) employees are paid below the market rate

   B) employees in the same job receive the same salary

   C) the starting salaries for new hires outpace year-to-year raises for existing staff

   D) international workers earn less than others due to cost of living

108. What is the level of probability that an organization may be exposed to a hazard or loss?

   A) risk

   B) adverse impact

   C) vulnerability

   D) loss analysis

109. Which of the following is true under ADEA?

   A) A company may not set a retirement age.

   B) A company may discontinue pension accruals for employees over age sixty-two.

   C) An employer may terminate an employee over forty for poor performance.

   D) It is against the law to require employees to be over eighteen.

110. A company wants to understand the attitudes of employees in a short amount of time. Which method would be most appropriate?

   A) observation

   B) in-person interview

   C) questionnaire

   D) hearsay

111. According to the ADA, a job description should list the essential functions of a job—

   A) in order of percentage of time spent on a task

   B) in order of importance

   C) in no order at all

   D) in alphabetical order

112. Which of the following laws protects people with physical or mental limitations from discrimination?

   A)   FMLA

   B)   ADA

   C)   ADEA

   D)   ERISA

113. What is a term used to describe when a qualified white male is denied an opportunity because preference is given to a member of a protected minority group?

   A)   reasonable accommodation

   B)   unfair employment practice

   C)   hostile work environment

   D)   reverse discrimination

114. Which of the following is considered indirect compensation?

   A)   use of a company cell phone

   B)   short-term disability insurance

   C)   401(k) matching contributions

   D)   all of the above

115. *Quid pro quo* refers to which of the following?

   A)   sexual harassment

   B)   workplace accommodations

   C)   orientation

   D)   whistleblowing

116. A workweek in which a full week's work is completed in fewer days is called—

   A)   a compressed workweek

   B)   telecommuting

   C)   job sharing

   D)   work-life balance

117. Which of the following is not an internal recruitment activity?

   A)   employee referrals

   B)   job posting on a website

   C)   job rotation

   D)   promoting from within

118. If your state minimum wage is higher than the federal minimum wage, how much are you required to pay employees at minimum?

   A)   state minimum wage

   B)   federal minimum wage

   C)   average of state and federal minimum wages

   D)   none of the above

119. Right-to-work laws allow states to—

   A)   ensure all citizens retain their jobs

   B)   require binding arbitration for disputes

   C)   require union membership at any company

   D)   prohibit compulsory union membership

120. Collective bargaining in which unions negotiate pay and working conditions similar to those that exist within the industry is referred to as which of the following?

   A)   multiple bargaining

   B)   parallel bargaining

   C)   coordinated bargaining

   D)   market bargaining

121. Which of the following decisions can be made on the basis of employee complaints?

   A)   Employees can be reassigned to other departments.

   B)   Managers can be fired.

   C)   The company can identify areas where improvements may be needed.

   D)   Management can hire more staff.

122. Which is not a stage of the organizational life cycle?

   A)   birth

   B)   growth

   C)   maturity

   D)   death

123. The Occupational Safety and Health Act (OSHA) was enacted in:

A) 1912

B) 1960

C) 1970

D) 1986

124. An employee with HIV/AIDS who can perform essential functions of her job and is not a threat to the safety of other employees is protected by:

A) EEOC

B) FLSA

C) ADA

D) ADEA

125. Which of the following is an informal process of dispute resolution used by the EEOC?

A) employment at will

B) conciliation

C) mandated benefits

D) reconciliation

126. Which of the following information is typically not included in a job description?

A) a list of responsibilities

B) FLSA status

C) required skills

D) company history

127. Which of the following does not usually affect recruitment planning?

A) government regulations

B) demographics of the workforce

C) available labor pool

D) location of the organization

128. Which of the following is a compensation philosophy that determines the value of the person's job in the organization and in the market?

A) market-based pay

B) pay for the person

C) pay for the job

D) equitable pay

129. Which agency oversees public sector labor relations?

A) National Labor Relations Board

B) Department of Labor

C) Federal Labor Relations Council

D) OFCCP

130. Which of the following is not a characteristic of an independent contractor?

A) They can work offsite.

B) They have flexibility to set their own work schedules.

C) They have an indefinite relationship with the employer.

D) They must use their own work tools.

131. Which is not a benefit of training?

A) reduced profits

B) reduction in errors

C) reduction in turnover

D) improved productivity

132. Which of the following best describes mentoring?

A) providing feedback to a subordinate regarding his or her performance on the job

B) a professional relationship between two people that involves advice and support

C) training a classroom of new hires on a product or service

D) shadowing a person to learn his or her job

133. A manager only hires young women as waitresses. What is this an example of?

    A) disparate treatment
    B) adverse impact
    C) harassment
    D) fair employment practice

134. How long do employers have to verify an employee's eligibility to work in the US?

    A) one day
    B) three days
    C) seven days
    D) fourteen days

135. What should be completed before writing a job description?

    A) candidate interview
    B) job analysis
    C) downsizing
    D) restructuring

136. A forced distribution method of rating employees does which of the following?

    A) It rates employees across a standard distribution.
    B) It ranks employees in order of productivity.
    C) It distributes 360 surveys to the employee's peers.
    D) It makes the employee rate him/herself.

137. State "right to work" laws prohibit which of the following?

    A) union shops
    B) termination of employment
    C) unfair labor practices
    D) formation of unions

138. Succession planning is important because it—

    A) ensures that key roles in the company will not be vacant
    B) provides feedback for all employees
    C) requires managers to go through training
    D) controls the company's operating budget

139. With respect to non-discrimination laws, which of the following is true?

    A) Federal laws trump state laws.
    B) Employers must follow the law that provides the greatest employee protection.
    C) State laws trump federal laws.
    D) none of the above

140. Strategic planning is centered around the organization's—

    A) staffing plan
    B) mission statement
    C) needs analysis
    D) competitor data

141. Which of the following questions should an employer not ask its applicants?

    A) Are you able to perform the essential functions of the job with or without reasonable accommodation?
    B) Are you able to work on Sundays?
    C) Are you a US citizen?
    D) Are you over eighteen years old?

142. Workers' compensation is regulated by which body?

    A) state government
    B) Department of Labor
    C) OFCCP
    D) NLRB

143. The ADEA prohibits discrimination against which age groups?

   A) people over eighteen years old

   B) people between twenty-one and sixty-five years old

   C) people between forty and sixty-five years old

   D) people over forty years old

144. Which of the following is examined during an environmental scan?

   A) turnover rate

   B) economic factors

   C) employee complaints

   D) organizational charts

145. Which of the following questions may an employer ask an applicant?

   A) Do you speak English fluently?

   B) What race are you?

   C) Are you married?

   D) Do you have a disability?

146. What did the McDonnell-Douglas Corp v. Green case establish?

   A) adverse impact

   B) unfair employment practices

   C) disparate treatment

   D) pregnancy non-discrimination

147. Career planning focuses on the needs of whom?

   A) employees

   B) managers

   C) the organization

   D) the owners

148. Which concept recognizes that employee productivity is directly related to job satisfaction?

   A) HR management

   B) strategic planning

   C) human relations

   D) performance management

149. Which theory states that people are motivated by rewards?

   A) equity theory

   B) expectancy theory

   C) Alderfer's ERG theory

   D) motivation-hygiene theory

150. An audit of the services and costs billed by healthcare providers is called:

   A) claims analysis

   B) utilization review

   C) performance guarantee

   D) pay for performance

1.	A)	39.	C)	77.	C)	115.	A)
2.	D)	40.	A)	78.	A)	116.	A)
3.	C)	41.	C)	79.	B)	117.	B)
4.	A)	42.	B)	80.	A)	118.	A)
5.	C)	43.	D)	81.	B)	119.	D)
6.	C)	44.	B)	82.	C)	120.	B)
7.	B)	45.	A)	83.	C)	121.	C)
8.	C)	46.	B)	84.	C)	122.	D)
9.	A)	47.	D)	85.	A)	123.	C)
10.	D)	48.	A)	86.	D)	124.	C)
11.	A)	49.	A)	87.	B)	125.	B)
12.	C)	50.	D)	88.	D)	126.	D)
13.	D)	51.	C)	89.	A)	127.	B)
14.	B)	52.	D)	90.	D)	128.	C)
15.	C)	53.	B)	91.	C)	129.	C)
16.	D)	54.	C)	92.	A)	130.	C)
17.	C)	55.	C)	93.	D)	131.	A)
18.	B)	56.	C)	94.	A)	132.	B)
19.	B)	57.	A)	95.	B)	133.	A)
20.	C)	58.	A)	96.	C)	134.	B)
21.	B)	59.	C)	97.	A)	135.	B)
22.	B)	60.	D)	98.	C)	136.	B)
23.	A)	61.	A)	99.	A)	137.	A)
24.	A)	62.	C)	100.	B)	138.	A)
25.	D)	63.	D)	101.	D)	139.	B)
26.	C)	64.	B)	102.	B)	140.	B)
27.	A)	65.	B)	103.	D)	141.	C)
28.	C)	66.	D)	104.	C)	142.	A)
29.	A)	67.	B)	105.	A)	143.	D)
30.	C)	68.	A)	106.	A)	144.	B)
31.	A)	69.	C)	107.	C)	145.	A)
32.	A)	70.	A)	108.	A)	146.	C)
33.	B)	71.	B)	109.	C)	147.	A)
34.	B)	72.	C)	110.	C)	148.	C)
35.	A)	73.	D)	111.	B)	149.	B)
36.	D)	74.	D)	112.	B)	150.	B)
37.	B)	75.	D)	113.	D)		
38.	C)	76.	B)	114.	D)		

REFERENCES

ONE: BUSINESS MANAGEMENT AND STRATEGY

[1] "Choose Your Business Structure," US Small Business Administration, accessed August 19, 2015, http://www.sba.gov/category/navigation-structure/starting-managing-business/starting-business/choose-your-business-stru.

[2] Sharon P. Brown, "Business Processes and Business Functions: a New Way of Looking at Employment," Monthly Labor Review, December 2008, 51-70, see US Department of Labor, Bureau of Labor Statistics, Office of Publications and Special Studies, accessed August 19, 2015, http://www.bls.gov/opub/mlr/2008/12/art3full.pdf.

[3] "Key Components of a Strategic Human Capital Plan," US Office of Personnel Management, Human Capital Management Reference Materials, accessed August 19, 2015, http://www.opm.gov/policy-data-oversight/human-capital-management/reference-materials/strategic-alignment/keycomponents.pdf.

TWO: WORKFORCE PLANNING AND EMPLOYMENT

[1] "Laws Enforced by E.E.O.C.," US Equal Employment Opportunity Commission, http://www.eeoc.gov/laws/statutes/ (accessed August 19, 2015).

[2] "Title VII of the Civil Rights Act of 1964," US Equal Employment Opportunity Commission, Civil Rights Act of 1964, Title VII, 42 U.S.C. §2000e (1964); http://www.eeoc.gov/laws/statutes/titlevii.cfm (accessed August 19, 2015)

[3] "The Pregnancy Discrimination Act of 1978," US Equal Employment Opportunity Commission, 42 U.S.C. §2000e(k) (1978); Pub. L. No. 95-555, 92 Stat. 2076 (1978); http://www.eeoc.gov/laws/statutes/pregnancy.cfm (accessed August 19, 2015).

[4] "The Equal Pay Act of 1963," US Equal Employment Opportunity Commission, 29 U.S.C. §206(d) (1963); Pub. L. No. 88-38 77 Stat. 56 (1963); http://www.eeoc.gov/laws/statutes/epa.cfm (accessed August 19, 2015).

[5] "The Age Discrimination in Employment Act of 1967 (ADEA)," US Equal Employment Opportunity Commission, 29 U.S.C. §621 (1967); Pub. L. No. 90-202, 81 Stat. 602 (1967); http://www.eeoc.gov/laws/statutes/adea.cfm (accessed August 19, 2015).

[6] "Title I of the Americans with Disabilities Act of 1990 (ADA)," US Equal Employment Opportunity Commission, 42 U.S.C. §12101 (1990); Pub. L. No. 101-336, 104 Stat. 327; http://www.eeoc.gov/laws/statutes/ada.cfm (accessed August 19, 2015).

[7] "The Genetic Information Non-discrimination Act of 2008 (GINA)," US Equal Employment Opportunity Commission, Pub. L. No. 110-233 122 Stat. 881 (2008); http://www.eeoc.gov/laws/statutes/gina.cfm (accessed August 19, 2015).

[8] "Hiring: Affirmative Action," US Department of Labor, http://www.dol.gov/dol/topic/hiring/affirmativeact.htm (accessed August 19, 2015).

[9] "Succession Planning Process," Human Capital Management Reference Materials, US Office of Personnel Management, https://www.opm.gov/policy-data-oversight/human-capital-management/reference-materials/leadership-knowledge-management/successionplanning.pdf, last modified September 2005.

[10] "Immigration Reform and Control Act of 1986," US Citizenship and Immigration Services, http://www.uscis.gov/tools/glossary/immigration-reform-and-control-act-1986-irca (accessed August 19, 2015) and Immigration Reform and Control Act of 1986, Pub. L. No. 99-603, 100 Stat. 3359 (1986); http://www.gpo.gov/fdsys/pkg/STATUTE-100/pdf/STATUTE-100-Pg3445.pdf (accessed August 19, 2015).

[11] "Temporary (Nonimmigrant) Workers," US Citizenship and Immigration Services, http://www.uscis.gov/working-united-states/temporary-workers/temporary-nonimmigrant-workers, last modified September 7, 2011.

[12] "Immigration Reform and Control Act of 1986," US Citizenship and Immigration Services, http://www.uscis.gov/tools/glossary/immigration-reform-and-control-act-1986-irca (accessed August 19, 2015) and Immigration Reform and Control Act of 1986, Pub. L. No. 99-603, 100 Stat. 3359 (1986); http://www.gpo.gov/fdsys/pkg/STATUTE-100/pdf/STATUTE-100-Pg3445.pdf (accessed August 19, 2015).

THREE: TOTAL REWARDS: COMPENSATION AND BENEFITS

[1] "Required Employee Benefits," US Small Business Administration, http://www.sba.gov/content/required-employee-benefits (accessed August 19, 2015).

[2] "About the Law," US Department of Health and Human Services, last modified August 13, 2015, http://www.hhs.gov/healthcare/rights/.

[3] "Mental Health Parity," US Department of Labor, accessed August 19, 2015, http://www.dol.gov/ebsa/mentalhealthparity/.

FIVE: EMPLOYEE AND LABOR RELATIONS

[1] "Summary of the Major Laws of the Department of Labor," US Department of Labor, Office of the Secretary, accessed August 19, 2015, http://www.dol.gov/opa/aboutdol/lawsprog.htm.

[2] Jelle Visser, "Union Membership Statistics in Twenty-Four Countries," Monthly Labor Review, January 2006, 38-49, see US Department of Labor, Bureau of Labor Statistics, Office of Publications and Special Studies, accessed August 19, 2015, http://www.bls.gov/opub/mlr/2006/01/art3full.pdf.

FREE VIDEO · FREE · FREE VIDEO

PHR Essential Test Tips Video from Trivium Test Prep!

Dear Customer,

Thank you for purchasing from Trivium Test Prep! We're honored to help you prepare for your PHR exam.

To show our appreciation, we're offering a **FREE *PHR Essential Test Tips* Video by Trivium Test Prep.*** Our video includes 35 test preparation strategies that will make you successful on the PHR. All we ask is that you email us your feedback and describe your experience with our product. Amazing, awful, or just so-so: we want to hear what you have to say!

To receive your **FREE *PHR Essential Test Tips* Video**, please email us at 5star@triviumtestprep.com. Include "Free 5 Star" in the subject line and the following information in your email:

1. The title of the product you purchased.
2. Your rating from 1 – 5 (with 5 being the best).
3. Your feedback about the product, including how our materials helped you meet your goals and ways in which we can improve our products.
4. Your full name and shipping address so we can send your **FREE *PHR Essential Test Tips* Video**.

If you have any questions or concerns please feel free to contact us directly at 5star@triviumtestprep.com.

Thank you!

- Trivium Test Prep Team

*To get access to the free video please email us at 5star@triviumtestprep.com, and please follow the instructions above.